Behind The Baton

Behind The Baton

A Who's Who of Conductors

ROBIN MAY

FREDERICK MULLER LIMITED
LONDON

First published in Great Britain 1981 by
Frederick Muller Limited, London NW2 6LE

Copyright © 1981 Robin May

British Library Cataloguing in Publication Data

  May, Robin
    Behind the baton.
    1. Conductors (Music) – Biography
    I. Title
    785'.092'2   ML402

  ISBN 0–584–10456–1

Typeset by Computacomp (UK) Ltd, Scotland
Printed in Great Britain by The Anchor Press
Ltd, Colchester, Essex

Picture acknowledgements

Claudio Abbado. By permission of Clive Barda. Sir John Barbirolli. By permission of Camera Press. Sir Thomas Beecham. By permission of E.M.I. Leonard Bernstein. By permission of C.B.S. Records/Clive Barda. Hans von Bülow. From a painting by Franz von Lenbach. Victor de Sabata. By permission of Decca. Antal Dorati. By permission of Phonogram. Wilhelm Furtwängler. By permission of E.M.I. Bernard Haitink. By permission of Phonogram. Eugen Jochum. By permission of Phonogram. Rudolf Kempe. By permission of Decca. Otto Klemperer. By permission of E.M.I. Kirill Kondrashin. By permission of Decca. James Levine. By permission of R.C.A./Clive Barda. Lorin Maazel. By permission of Decca. Zubin Mehta. By permission of C.B.S. Records. Artur Nikisch. Author's collection. Seiji Ozawa. By permission of Alex 'Tug' Wilson. Simon Rattle. By permission of E.M.I./Clive Barda. Tullio Serafin. By permission of E.M.I. Sir Georg Solti. By permission of Decca. Leopold Stokowski. By permission of R.C.A./Clive Barda. Arturo Toscanini. By permission of R.C.A. Felix Weingartner. Author's collection. Sir Henry Wood. Author's collection.

Vaughan Williams once shouted at me – along with hundreds of other Berkshire schoolchildren. He was dissatisfied with our interpretation of his stirring arrangements of folk songs. There will be no more personal name-dropping in this book …

Introduction and Acknowledgements

Though most of this book consists of an A to Z of conductors, two extra chapters have been added, mainly to set them in their historical context and show how their unique and often controversial profession came about and developed.

The first chapter contains some general remarks about conductors and conducting, followed by a brief study of the birth of the profession up to the second half of the last century, at which point the Who's Who section takes up the story.

In it, 575 conductors, living and dead, are considered, some of the very famous ones being described in short essays. The list could have been stretched to several thousands, though – in a book of this size – only if all the entries were in barebones form. That mine of information, the *British Music Yearbook* (1980), contains a list of well over 500 conductors based in Britain and/or bookable through British concert agents, including many, alas, who cannot be included here for reasons of space. For the reader will surely wish to know of past as well as present glories. Names like Toscanini, Beecham and a score more live on vividly, and not simply because of recordings of varying quality. They live on as men and as legends.

After the *Who's Who* chapter comes a series of relevant quotations about some early giants down to Wagner, then there is a short, personal discography, short because the Niagara of recordings that appear each year make it absurd to attempt anything except a small list when there are so many current guides available in book and magazine form.

The newcomer to music, and to the histrionics or otherwise of conductors, should if possible join any society run by a leading orchestra that enables him or her to attend rehearsals, for they are where the real work is done. There have been exceptions, of course. The incomparable Beecham could demand – and achieve – a very different interpretation of a piece in performance, and his own players could always give it him.

On a personal note, I was fortunate in that, as a drama student at the Central School of Speech and Drama, which was then situated in nooks and crannies of the Albert Hall's upper regions, I could attend rehearsals regularly. In those days it was still London's leading concert hall, the change to the Festival Hall coming half way through my period at Central, which was from 1950 to 1953. Today's students have far better facilities in Swiss Cottage, but are not exposed to regular musical glories.

The school had rooms and a small theatre (now a restaurant) on the amphitheatre level and a few rooms lower down. Though no one missed an acting class, less inspiring subjects could be skipped by music-loving students, who would creep into the amphitheatre seats. How could one resist such an opportunity? The roster below included Furtwängler, Koussevitzky, Beecham and, indeed, nearly every conductor of note except Toscanini, whose only post-war appearance was at the Festival Hall.

Particularly vivid is the memory of a Beethoven cycle in 1951, with Josef Krips rehearsing the London Symphony Orchestra. Even his vast bald head seemed to smile. Much admired by his players, he was tough and demanding, 'tyrannical' according to one of the anonymous contributors to the admirable book *Orchestra*, which consists of comments by orchestral players – all named except in one very frank section – plus an introduction by André Previn. The tyrannical side of Krips did not reach up as far as the amphitheatre, though he looked tough despite his beams. Once, the composer Robert Stolz was on the podium. The beams were broader than ever, as Krips, beside himself with joy at the Viennese schmaltz, stood smiling in the gangway beside the orchestra, listening to his musicians playing the light music of his fatherland.

My one regret from those days is that I never attended a rehearsal of the matchless Victor de Sabata, a conductor whose career, shortened by ill-health, was overshadowed by that of the glamorous Toscanini. In *Orchestra* de Sabata gets his due. According to Hugh Maguire he was the greatest, most musical conductor that he ever came across, absolutely overwhelming ...

In those heady days just after the war – the late '40s and early '50s – London was a paradise for newcomers and old musical hands alike. In the aftermath of war – a war in which music had boomed in Britain –

giants of the past vied with rising stars from overseas in appearing in London. *The* English orchestra at that time was the London Philharmonic, which I heard in 1947 in a complete cycle of the Beethoven symphonies conducted by de Sabata. I heard Bruno Walter conducting the same orchestra. Regretfully, I cannot claim to have been present at Toscanini's post-war appearance – at the Festival Hall in two all-Brahms programmes with the Philharmonia – though I have a vivid memory of a packed Albert Hall, the Philharmonia, the legendary Dinu Lipatti playing Grieg, and Herbert von Karajan, then virtually unknown in Britain, conducting *Don Juan* and Beethoven's Fifth. All this and the Proms and other concerts, too.

I never had a chance to attend an opera rehearsal in those days. In the late '40s, the New London Opera Company at the Cambridge Theatre was pre-eminent until it could no longer compete with the subsidized companies. Its founder, Jay Pomeroy, was ruined. Covent Garden was painfully building a native company up from scratch, and there was far better opera to be had at Sadler's Wells. The Welsh National Opera had already started its long climb to the immense prestige it attained in the '70s, Glyndebourne resumed its festivals in 1950, but Scottish Opera was presumably not even a gleam in Sir Alexander Gibson's eye.

There are many conductors in this book, including some I heard in the late '40s and early '50s, who may be unknown to the concertgoer who has the misfortune not to love opera. Happily, most of the world's great conductors are addicted to it. The operatic conductor has to cope with so many more problems than the orchestral conductor, who can be so easily carried along by his orchestra. True, the operatic maestro can also be carried along by his orchestra, but he is in action on all fronts – the singers, the chorus, off-stage forces. However much assistance he may have from his troops he is finally responsible. Even when an over-powerful producer – brilliant, average, bad or monstrous – has dominated the proceedings to the extent of casting the opera, an occurrence more common in Europe than in Britain as yet, the man in the pit is still the key figure artistically, however stellar the cast; and in a new production, he will be rehearsing the singers from the piano after their period with the opera coaches, or répétiteurs.

So many European conductors started as coaches, and with more opera in Britain and America than ever before, this happy situation is to be found virtually throughout the operatic world. One of the problems the young conductor has to face is how to get hold of a group of players to conduct. Though he is unlikely to be let loose in the opera house, except in an emergency, in his very early days, the essential routine of coaching, conducting off-stage choirs or bands and other tasks will help him become ready for his chance. He must, of course, *be* ready for it, as the cellist Toscanini was ready when he stepped in to take over a performance of *Aida* in Rio de Janeiro in 1886 after the regular conductor had been on the receiving end of a demonstration. Opera, for all the occasional catastrophes and miscastings, the vagaries of producers and the variable standard of acting, can reach heights beyond anything else in the performing arts. And, whatever the rival claims of voice and staging, only when the conductor and his players are inspired can the full glory occur.

There are comparatively few books about the history of conducting. There is a short bibliography at the end of this book, but I must acknowledge more fully three which have been most instructive, apart from *Orchestra*. That is so valuable because it is musicians talking, amplifying and confirming the things I have heard musician friends say. My thanks to Macdonald and Jane's for allowing me to quote from it.

The first of the three books is Harold C. Schonberg's *The Great Conductors*, which, apart from being a mine of informed comment as well as historical fact, is also very entertaining. The second book is *Conductor's World* by David Wooldridge, the composer-conductor. This is a more technical book and has been most helpful. Only the author's evident lack of sympathy with Italian opera makes it a less than complete record. The third is an earlier book, Adam Carse's masterly, *The Orchestra from Beethoven to Berlioz*, which is not only a work of great scholarship, but also a source of useful quotations which have greatly assisted me with section three of this book.

Special acknowledgement must be made to the enormous eighth edition of the *International Who's Who in Music* and to that most accurate of operatic encyclopedias, the second edition of *The Concise Oxford Dictionary of Opera*, edited by Harold Rosenthal and John Warrack.

I owe a debt to the many artists' agents who sent me information about their clients, and to the individual conductors who resolved my queries. The publicity departments of the London Philharmonic Orchestra, the London Symphony Orchestra, the Bournemouth Symphony Orchestra, the Philharmonia, and the Royal Opera, Covent

Garden, were especially helpful among the organizations I contacted, as were the promotional departments of the record companies. As to the musicians who have expressed strong opinions to me down the years, I hope I will be excused from revealing their names.

Yet in the end the author-compiler of a book crammed with hundreds of short biographies must take full responsibility for what he writes. There are moments of despair when one knows that a conductor's contribution to *Who's Who* or wherever is inaccurate and that other books contradict each other as well, but a compiler does his best to ferret out the truth. (One eminent conductor, who spent a number of years in ballet, had a very different life, apparently, from that presented in two leading ballet encyclopedias, and even they, not surprisingly, do not entirely agree.)

One final word: I have tried in the biographical entries to present a consensus of opinion, though my own opinions show through from time to time. Yet there can never be a true consensus. The two extremes of great conducting might be said to be that of Furtwängler and Toscanini, and their musical ancestors, Wagner and Berlioz, the former in each case being extremely flexible in his tempos. Some may cherish Furtwängler this side of idolatry, others Toscanini, but it is an unfortunate music lover who cannot respond to both. There is no World's Greatest Conductor at any given time, though von Karajan's warmest admirers will tell you differently. There is no world's worst either, though most orchestral players would put forward a candidate.

Robin May
Wimbledon, 1980

The Conductor

Someone has to do it. There have, of course, been orchestras without conductors, the best known being a Russian one five years after the Revolution. However, without a man and a baton to guide, misguide, bore or inspire them, the band of brothers began to look more and more to their leader. The experiment foundered.

Robert A. Simon, the American music critic, faced with another such orchestra in New York in the 1920s, concisely summed up the situation: he found that an orchestra of able musicians could do better without a conductor at all than with a bad one.

Naïve newcomers to the concert hall, or those watching a giant sweating face on TV, often imagine that the conductor is doing it all and that without his guidance there would be chaos. Players can hero worship a great conductor as well as any listener, but they are 'members of the toughest and most sensitive professional tribe the arts have ever known', as the late Charles Reid put it. If a new man proves inadequate at the first rehearsal, the leader or one of the principals may take him aside and say, so Raymond Clark tells us in *Orchestra*: 'We've always played it this way, and we shall go on playing it this way'. It may, of course, result in very good reviews for the new young hopeful.

Today's conductors are inevitably more democratic than their predecessors, some of whom were undoubtedly tyrants. Certain things do not change, however. Though players are never going to fall below a certain standard – they have their professional pride even in the face of rankest incompetence – they have always been able to make life difficult or even impossible for a conductor during rehearsals.

Franz Strauss, the horn-playing father of Richard Strauss, and the doyen of all orchestral conductor baiters down the years, summed up his philosophy in these memorable words:

> You conductors who are so proud of your power! When a new
> man faces the orchestra – from the way he walks up the steps
> of the podium and opens his score – before he even picks up
> his baton – we know whether he is the master or we.

How can a conductor face up to such scrutiny? He must have
personality as well as deep knowledge, and he must have powers of
leadership. He must have what Kent saw in Lear's countenance –
authority. Musicianship and stick technique are not enough.

Long lectures will do him no good. Klemperer was a notorious pre-
rehearsal talker in his American years, so much so that the oboist of the
New York Philharmonic, Bruno Labate, as minute as Klemperer was
monumental, once rose to his feet and said: 'Klemp, you talka too
much.'

As for stick technique, it is not all important. The conductor is the
focal point for the orchestra, or he should be, and his baton and how he
uses it is unarguably a matter of musical moment. Yet there have been
great conductors, most notably Furtwängler whose beat was
incomprehensible. No one could claim that Reginald Goodall's gestures
are easy to follow, yet his Wagnerian performances are usually
triumphant because his players respond to his vision.

Histrionics on the podium are crosses orchestras have to bear, though
when they happen in performance when they have been absent in
rehearsals, it at least allows players some cynical chuckles. Some of the
finest conductors, Richard Strauss among them, have or have had tiny
beats, some have not, some use no baton. It is a matter of temperament.

As important as the beat are the eyes, some would say much more so,
notably those who played with Beecham. His eyes were everywhere and
everyone saw them, whereas lesser conductors attract less attention.
From a music desk you can see as much as you want to see, hence the old
story of the player who ran into a friend after a concert. 'Who was the
conductor?' asked the friend. 'Didn't notice,' said the musician.

Perhaps the best summing up of the relative importance of stick and
the whole man is Hugh Magguire's. In *Orchestra*, he is quoted as
questioning whether he has ever looked at a conductor's beat in his life
and not being sure, then saying: 'One looks at the conductor, the whole
man. The message comes from the balls of the feet, right through to the
top of the head, not just what he does with his hands.'

Beecham was a supreme example of this. Not for him a final rehearsal. As noted in the introduction, the actual performance might be very different from the rehearsals; and because he was trusted and loved by his players, they would revel in the risks. Malcolm Arnold, a trumpet player before he was a composer, recalls that Beecham had the ability to make a player feel that what he was doing was really worthwhile and that he 'had the capacity for giving a player confidence to take enormous risks in his playing'.

Are orchestral players therefore the best judge of a conductor's worth? Of course. That does not mean that all are agreed all the time, besides which personality enters into it. Sir Malcolm Sargent was technically able, but highly unpopular with players for most of his career. Players may argue about excellence, just as actors argue about the relative merits of Gielgud and Olivier, for example, but all tend to agree as to who are the duds. The arguments can be instructive and amusing to outsiders. The author had two friends in the Covent Garden orchestra in Solti's reign in the 1960s. Their views of him were diametrically opposed, though it must be stressed that the anti-Solti player was not suggesting that he was a dud. Similarly, in a restaurant near the Festival Hall two musicians, one young and one middle-aged, were discussing the merits of a Rumanian conductor who is a legend in his own lifetime. The older player, who had served under a number of legends was merely prepared to agree that he thought the Rumanian was very fine, but he hadn't finally made up his mind. The younger player, growing more apoplectic every moment, clearly considered him the ultimate maestro. It was a cheering conversation for eavesdroppers, a reminder that there is no final word.

The jet age and a vast increase in the number of concerts has resulted in an increased number of conductors, with far fewer staying for a period of years, decades even, with the same orchestra. The long term conductor, given enough talent, can give his orchestra a distinct personality, yet one can understand those players who prefer new faces for the variety of musical stimulation offered.

The major conductors will make players excel themselves. They know their musicians are familiar or even over-familiar with most of the repertoire and they will spend much time in rehearsal balancing the orchestra, not, as John Ronayne has said, 'by talking but by indications of hand, eye or body, and by force of character.' In that way they 'tuned the orchestra in rehearsal' and had a 'fresh and eager instrument' for the concert.

Balance is not easily achieved. The theatre director can judge effect by moving about the auditorium but the conductor must know from experience the effect his orchestra are making in the body of the hall. Stokowski used to get round the problem in Philadelphia by initially having his assistant conduct during rehearsals at first so that he could sit at the back of the hall and judge the sound from there. Unfortunately, the science of acoustics is still very inexact, so much so that some modern halls are far less suited to music-making than buildings of the 19th and 18th centuries.

All conductors have to face the fact that, especially in major musical centres, orchestras know the standard concert and operatic repertoire very well indeed. Fortunately, as the last century wore on, orchestral parts grew more and more rewarding for players. Dazzling challenges were offered them by Richard Strauss, Stravinsky, Mahler and others in the early 20th century. However, Beethoven remains the most steadily popular of composers with the public. Not with orchestral musicians, however, who have to play the symphonies far too often, and can be heard venting their wrath on the composer, who, from a purely playing point of view, offers them far less enjoyment than many lesser composers. 'Not the bloody Emperor/Seventh/Eroica again!' For some players the situation is worse than for others. The wretched trumpeters suffer most. The unvalved trumpets of Mozart's and Beethoven's day were primitive enough for them to be used only very rarely for solo passages while for the whole orchestra, seemingly unending repetitions of the famous works are demoralizing enough to make a young or not-so-young conductor's task a daunting one. Indeed, to hear two musicians talking about Beethoven the symphonist can sometimes be like listening to two actors complaining about the one or two-dimensional parts provided for them by the average thriller writer and the boredom that ensues. The actors have only their pay to look forward to: the players can look forward to a Klemperer, a de Sabata, a Giulini, to restore their faith.

In the last resort, it must be stressed that the conductor has chosen his profession, one that can bring even a modest talent fame and far more money than any orchestral player. As for the occasional humiliations, if you can't stand the heat, stay out of the kitchen.

The vast majority of the conductors recorded later in this book are sincere, dedicated men, unlike the sort described by Robert Schumann in 1836, when modern conducting had only just been born. He warned his readers in the *Neue Zeitschrift für Musik* of the 'vanity and self-importance of the conductors who do not want to relinquish the baton, partly because they want to be constantly before the audience, partly to hide the fact that a competent orchestra can take care of itself without their leadership.' Schumann died before the conductor cult had really begun. Yet the origins of conducting go back far earlier than the 19th century, and therefore, a short history of the conductor may help to set the biographies, short and long, in perspective.

The conductor as we know him has existed for a century and a half, but his origins go back much further. Just how far is uncertain, for time-beating is a very ancient occupation. No doubt someone was beating time with his hand and/or foot for a Greek choir on the ringing plains of windy Troy. The poet Horace was doing just that for maidens and youths in Roman times, and no doubt also there was some time-beating among the wandering minstrels of the Dark Ages. From the early Middle Ages the references begin again.

Some of these time-beaters presumably engaged in interpretation. In pre-baton days, the beat could be given by a hand or hands, a roll of paper, a fist, the head or sometimes a stick. The transition from mere time-beater must have been made by composers with authority and personality to match. Monteverdi was certainly a conductor, though we know little of his methods. Thirty-eight instruments are listed at the start of the score of his *Orfeo*, first staged in 1607 in Mantua just ten years after opera itself had literally been invented in Florence.

However he operated, the composer-conductor – Monteverdi and his successors – was undoubtedly in charge of orchestra and singers alike, and it should be noted that well into our own century many great conductors were also composers, an admirable state of affairs whether the conductor was a good composer or not.

We know how Lully operated at the court of Louis XIV. He used a long ballet-master's cane, imposing uniform bowing on his famous string orchestra. He was mortally wounded in action, alas, for he accidentally stamped his cane down on his foot with such vigour that, according to some accounts, the cane went right through it. The result was a fatal gangrenous wound.

For most of the 18th century two conductors worked together with the ensemble or orchestra. One was a violinist, a leader indeed, who was in charge of the ensemble, the other, known as a conductor, was in charge of the rhythmic function from a keyboard instrument. This clavierist set tempos, cued orchestra and singers, beat time with one or both hands when not too busy providing harmonies or melodies, and was expected to save the day when things went wrong. Most music was made in this way until the 1830s, execution being the object of the twin commanders, rather than interpretation in the modern sense.

Yet it cannot always have been joint rule, for a strong-minded composer must have dominated the proceedings just as Monteverdi and Lully and others had done. Bach was as tough as Toscanini, once tearing off his wig and flinging it at a musician, roaring: 'You should have been a shoemaker!' He ruled from the leader's seat or the clavier.

No doubt other great composers of the period were almost as sure of themselves publicly, but few have been so vividly portrayed in print as Bach was by Johann Matthias Gesner, who wrote about him in 1738 conducting in a manner not very different from today's conductors:

> If you could see him ... presiding over thirty or forty musicians all at once, controlling this one with a nod, another by the stamp of a foot, a third with a warning finger, keeping time and tune, giving a high note to one, a low note to another, and notes between to some. This one man, standing alone in the midst of loud sounds, having the hardest task of all, can discern at every moment if anyone goes astray, and can keep all the musicians in order, restore any waverer to certainty and prevent him going wrong. Rhythm is in his every limb, he takes in all the harmonies by his subtle ear and utters the different parts through the medium of his own voice.

As is well known, Handel grabbed the soprano Cuzzoni on one occasion and threatened to throw her out of a window for refusing to sing an aria in *Ottone* as he had written it, while Gluck, a much less pleasant man than Handel, treated his players worse than Bach. He would make them repeat passages endlessly until they got them as he wanted, meanwhile being so rude that the Austrian Emperor had to step in on occasion. He once, we are told, brought a double bass player and his instrument to the floor by creeping up on him and administering a vicious pinch to his calf.

If few tried to achieve perfection so sadistically as Gluck, the objective was worthy enough. And by now it was possible, for there was one renowned orchestra, the Mannheim, which proved it regularly in performance. Some forty-five strong in the 1750s, it was then conducted from the leader's desk by the violinist Johann Stamitz, and the orchestra's influence was inspirational and colossal.

The Mozarts, father and seven-year-old son, heard the orchestra in 1763, father declaring it the best in Europe. Meanwhile, Haydn was the very demanding, although not tyrannical, Kapellmeister to Prince Esterházy, usually conducting from the clavier. He had only twenty-four players in his superb orchestra, though in London he had nearly twice as many and on one occasion as many as sixty.

Mozart was inevitably a brilliant conductor, demanding, of course, but happiness itself when things went well. The Irish tenor, Michael Kelly, in the cast of the première of *Le Nozze de Figaro* in Vienna in 1786 – he was Basilio and Curzio – has left us a most vivid and affecting memory of the occasion, and of Mozart as composer-conductor:

> All the original performers had the advantage of the instruction of the composer, who transfused into their minds his inspired meaning. I shall never forget his little animated countance, when lighted up with the glowing rays of genius –
> it is as impossible to describe as it would be to paint sunbeams.

It seems that Mozart did beat time normally from the keyboard. Sometimes it would appear that he conducted from a score, not an instrument. Or did he? Like so much early conducting history, we are left with tantalizing references to events, but are left guessing as to what exactly the references mean. It is possible that by now some conductors were more concerned with using *both* hands to conduct than with playing the clavier.

Beethoven was notoriously a dreadful conductor, simply because he was determined to continue conducting despite his advancing deafness. As everyone knows, he was still nominally in command at the first performance of the Ninth Symphony, where at one point he was 'shown' the applause by the contralto, Caroline Unger.

Poor Beethoven hardly helped his own cause. His relationships with his players were uneasy from the start, and after the onset of his deafness, he caused more harm than good. Viennese players used to hope devoutly that he would keep away. Yet, tragically, behind his weird, violent movements can be perceived the forerunner of the modern virtuoso conductor, moulding the orchestra to express what he believes is the composer's will. His gestures, his very body, were employed to force his will on his players. His tempos seem to have fluctuated in a way that was acceptable in the last century, but not in our own. Yet the curse of his deafness has resulted in Beethoven the conductor, who should have been the first of the moderns, presented in the pages of musical history as a performer of tragi-farce. Spohr wrote of one such moment during the first performance of the Seventh Symphony. After describing how the composer had practically crawled under the desk to indicate a piano section in the first movement, he went on thus:

> With the oncoming crescendo he became visible again, rising higher and higher and leaping into the air at that moment when, according to his calculations, the forte should have been reached. When the forte failed to materialize, he looked round in amazement, then stared incredulously at the orchestra, which was still playing piano. He got his bearings with the arrival of the forte, something that he could hear.

Beethoven died in 1827, a time when the orchestra was becoming the glorious blend of sounds it is today. Instruments were more efficient. By 1835, valve horns were being produced and, with both brass and woodwind becoming keyed instruments, intonation was improved and they were easier to play. Orchestras as a whole were getting bigger, with more strings, much to the joy of composers, the process being virtually complete by around 1850, by which time the era of the modern conductor had begun.

Orchestras were still basically opera orchestras, for there were few concert halls and public concerts until the middle of the 19th century. Audiences at all the performing arts were notoriously unruly on occasions, though the theatre suffered more than opera; players were not only badly paid in most orchestras, but, cellists excepted, had to stand to perform. Against this background the man with the baton arrived to take sole charge. It was high time.

For divided leadership, even allowing for the less complex scores of the 18th century, could never be ideal unless a very strong composer was present. No wonder orchestras, some of them very bad indeed, became hopelessly muddled. There was also the extra noise involved, audiences as well as players having to listen sometimes to leaders stamping or even clapping their hands. And on occasion pianist and violinist-conductor disagreed.

For all the confused evidence, there is no doubt that the baton was sometimes used in the 18th century, as was a rolled-up piece of paper, a technique used by the 'conductor' of the Sistine Choir in the 15th century, who sometimes wielded a short stick. Most revolutionary of all was Johann Friedrich Reichardt, a violinist, pianist and writer who became Kapellmeister in Berlin. Not only did he direct his singers and orchestra from a desk near the footlights placed in the centre of the orchestra, but he dispensed with the piano. He may or may not have used a baton, but he wanted the control later conductors expected by right.

The composer Spohr is usually credited with spreading the use of the baton through Europe, having previously wielded a violin, then a roll of paper. The paper – it was widely observed – made no noise. That was in 1810, and his graduation to the baton had the same advantage of silence.

'Why didn't we think of it before?' must have been the general consensus of opinion after the first shock, though Spohr has left us an account of what happened when he tried his idea out on the orchestra of the London Philharmonic Society in 1820. The famous account is usually weakened by not being given in full, as Adam Carse observed in his *The Orchestra from Beethoven to Berlioz*. It is of such exceptional interest that it deserves full treatment.

> Meanwhile my turn had come to direct one of the Philharmonic concerts, and I had created no less sensation than with my solo play. It was at that time still the custom there that when symphonies and overtures were performed, the pianist had the score before him, not exactly to conduct from it, but only to read after and play in with the orchestra at pleasure, which when it was heard, had a very bad effect. The

real conductor was the first violin, who gave the tempi, and now and then when the orchestra began to falter gave the beat with the bow of his violin. So numerous an orchestra, standing so far apart from each other as that of the Philharmonic, could not possibly go exactly together, and in spite of the excellence of the individual members, the ensemble was much worse than we are accustomed to in Germany. I had therefore resolved when my turn came to direct, to make an attempt to remedy this defective system. Fortunately at the morning rehearsal on the day when I was to conduct the concert, Mr Ries took the place at the piano, and he readily assented to give up the score to me and to remain wholly excluded from all participation in the performance. I then took my stand with the score at a separate music desk in front of the orchestra, drew my directing baton from my coat pocket and gave the signal to begin. Quite alarmed at such a novel procedure, some of the directors would have protested against it; but when I besought them to grant me at least one trial, they became pacified. The symphonies and overtures that were to be rehearsed were well known to me, and in Germany I had already directed at their performance. I therefore could not only give the tempi in a very decisive manner, but indicated also to the wind instruments and horns all their entries, which ensured them a confidence such as hitherto they had not known there. I also took the liberty, when the execution did not satisfy me, to stop, and in a very polite but earnest manner to remark upon the manner of execution, which remarks Mr. Ries at my request interpreted to the orchestra. Incited thereby to more than usual attention, and conducted with certainty by the *visible* manner of giving the time, they played with a spirit and a correctness such as till then they had never been heard to play with. Surprised and inspired by this result the orchestra immediately after the first part of the symphony, expressed aloud its collective assent to the new mode of conducting, and thereby overruled all further opposition on the part of the directors. In the vocal pieces also, the conducting of which I assumed at the request of Mr. Ries, particularly in the recitative, the leading with the baton, after I had explained the meaning of my movements, was completely successful, and the singers repeatedly expressed to me their satisfaction for the precision with which the orchestra now followed them.

The result in the evening was still more brilliant than I could have hoped for. It is true, the audience were at first startled by the novelty, and were seen whispering together; but when the music began and the orchestra executed the well-known symphony with unusual power and precision, the general approbation was shewn immediately on the conclusion of the first part by a long-sustained clapping of hands. The triumph of the baton as a time-giver was decisive, and no one was seen any more seated at a piano during the performance of symphonies and overtures.

In fact, the Philharmonic Society was not yet completely rid of pianists and violinist-leaders, but their days were numbered. Spohr was writing from memory in 1847, and, indeed, the critic Arthur Jacobs, noting that Carse gives May 8 as the great day and Myles Foster, historian of the Royal Philharmonic Society, gives April 10, researched the matter, deciding that Spohr actually used the baton only at the rehearsal of the third concert of the series. As critics and the ordinary public were allowed to attend, it was virtually a concert performance, which might explain Spohr's lapse. The matter remains undecided, but surely not the manner of the historic event.

Spohr also helped matters by (probably) being the first to have reference numbers and letters included in both score and orchestral parts. Until his time, if a conductor wanted to draw a player's or the whole orchestra's attention to a particular bar, there was a hiatus while everyone had to count bars. Thanks to Spohr, 'Two bars after Number Seven' was enough.

Naturally, it took some years for the broad principles of modern conducting to be established. Strangely the actual position of the conductor was still not standardized. Until around the middle of the century an opera conductor was likely to face the singers and have his back to his orchestra, turning to them from time to time. He would be stationed just beyond the prompter's box, though one French conductor, Jean Jacques Grasset, stood at the far end of the Paris Opéra orchestra. Some conductors actually faced the audience.

As now, baton lengths varied, and some were on the exotic side, none more so than Jullien's which was 22 inches long and bejewelled with gold, including golden serpents, and diamonds. Yet the profession as we know it was now gradually being established, and by the 1840s there were conductors, notable and not so notable, at work in leading cities all over Europe. Many are noted in the Who's Who section of this book, but some brief notes are needed before embarking on that.

Few of today's leading conductors are composers – with the notable exception of Boulez and Bernstein – yet as has been stressed, in the early days of conducting as we know it the two jobs usually went together. Spohr was regarded as a great composer in his own day, and the most notable conductors of that day were almost all leading composers: Weber, Spontini, Mendelssohn, Berlioz and Wagner. A rare exception was François-Antoine Habeneck, whose Conservatoire Orchestra in Paris was a revelation to all who heard it. He was not a composer, but a remarkable conductor (with a bow) of Beethoven and he played scores as written, not a common feature of his day. Berlioz was to claim that Habeneck deliberately tried to sabotage his *Requiem*, the composer saving the day by leaping to his feet to give the beat and guide orchestra and choir. In fact, it seems to have been a lapse, partly brought about by Habeneck's habit of conducting from the first violin part, instead of a full score. He can have had little realization of the problems involved in the stupendous work, and, indeed, does not seem to have responded much to 'new' music. Berlioz himself, with his immense knowledge of the orchestra, was a far greater conductor than Habeneck, yet the young Wagner was among those who admired the older man's interpretations of the Beethoven symphonies.

Weber was a man of the theatre and most of his conducting was in the opera house. He was a hard taskmaster, demanding the highest standards in Prague (where his men could swear at him in Czech) and Dresden. Quiet and undemonstrative, with a clear and precise beat, he reorganized the orchestra's position into something like the modern seating plans. Like Wagner after him, he believed in flexible tempos, as did Mahler and Furtwängler after them. Berlioz was noted for the strictness of his beat, while Toscanini in the same tradition was not prepared to relent tempos except when the score demanded it.

As for Spontini, the Napoleon of the orchestra, he was as hard a taskmaster as Weber, but far, far more flamboyant. A brilliant conductor of his own works, his attempts at the music of others was not so admired. Extremely short-sighted, he nevertheless was a grand conductor with his eyes. 'Like a king' he would stride into his orchestra, noted the German musician, Moritz Hanemann, then he would take up his field-marshal's position and look round with his piercing eyes. 'My left eye is for the first violins, my right eye the second violins,' he informed an impressed Wagner, while another admirer recalled a *forte* like a hurricane, piano like a whisper, *crescendo* to make one open one's eyes wider, *decrescendo* to give the effect of magical exhaustion and a *sforzando* to waken the dead.

The likeable Mendelssohn, who conducted with his body as well as his baton, according to his biographer Lampadius, was a lively conductor, classical by instinct and, though firm, a believer in teamwork and friendliness with his men.

Then, as now, conductors had very definite views about each other. Just as the listener can rejoice in Berlioz and Wagner, so he or she can enjoy the finest conductors of their 'rival' schools. But the executants with their fierce inner vision are less tolerant. As lovers of *Les Troyens* know, Berlioz was essentially a classicist, for all his vast orchestral dreams and themes, whereas Wagner was an arch romantic. Said Berlioz of Wagner, the conductor: 'His style is like dancing on a slack wire, *sempre tempo rubato*.' Whereas Wagner was to write of Berlioz's performance of the Mozart G minor Symphony, which he heard him conduct in London in 1855: 'I ... was amazed to find a conductor, who was so energetic in the interpretation of his own compositions, sink into the commonest rut of the vulgar timebeater.' Let it be noted that J. W. Davison, critic of *The Times*, wrote of that same performance: 'Mr. Berlioz, whose general conception of the symphony would have proved him, had proof been wanting, one of the greatest and most intelligent of conductors.'

This is an excellent reminder that, there is always more than one 'correct' way of interpreting a masterpiece, and that the informed amateur need not be shy of having a firm opinion. He will usually be in good company.

After the first glory brigade of conductors had shown what could be done, a new breed arrived on the scene. The composer-conductor remained a vital part of music making until our own century, most notably Richard Strauss and Mahler, yet by their time the solely interpretative conductors were dominating the scene. True, many of them, among them Weingartner and Klemperer, were also composers, and the reader will note in the main section of the book just how many of today's conductors are composers. But from the time of Hans von Bülow the interpretative conductor has gained the ascendancy. Bülow's father-in-law, Liszt, was primarily a composer, though a fine conductor too. Bülow was a great conductor (also a magnificent pianist).

Like the conductors who followed him, Bülow was greatly concerned with new music, as were Toscanini, Furtwängler, Beecham, Koussevitzky and Klemperer for much or most of their careers. Not all new music, of course, but the performance of new music was a natural, and inevitable part of their job. Few of today's leading conductors are much concerned with new works, which are usually left to young conductors or to specialists. It may be, as Peter Heyworth has suggested, that since 1918 the centre of creative gravity has moved away from the great symphony orchestra. Yet surely it must also be that most modern music has for the first time in musical history lost its hold on all but a small minority. And, naturally, most conductors would rather conduct what is wanted; and many of them would choose to conduct that anyway.

In the last resort, as in all great art, creative or interpretative, it is for the individual to decide. It is surely hard for most of today's Berliozians to imagine that any living conductor better possesses the talisman to the composer's heady, restrained, sensuous romanticism, his classical exuberance, and his controlled, yet breathtakingly exuberant rhythms, than Sir Colin Davis. Yet anyone not eager to hear other interpretations, perhaps equally valid, perhaps wretchedly mistaken in the event, must surely be blinding himself to one of the many joys of music.

A Who's Who of Conductors

Several points must be made about some of the entries on German conductors ...

The word Generalmusikdirektor means chief music director, and it refers to the senior musician in a German opera house. Not only is the holder of the imposing title the chief conductor, but he is also responsible for deciding musical policy, including which works will be given. He is also in charge of staffing.

The word Kapellmeister – 'chapel master' – used to refer to the choir master in a court chapel, but as, the 19th century progressed, was widely used as another word for a conductor.

When the name of a city is used in an entry on a German, or, indeed, on a conductor of one of the other very opera-orientated central European nations, it can be assumed that he was or is in charge of the city's main opera houses. Transfers are more frequent in the operatic league than in the British football league, so writing 'Ulm (1927–34)' – von Karajan's period there – is a space-saving way of getting information across.

It is impossible here to explain each change in the names of certain leading German opera houses down the years, but the reader may find it useful to remember that in Berlin today there are three leading houses, the Deutsche Oper in West Berlin (which was called the Städtische for many years) and, in East Berlin, the Staatsoper unter den Linden, referred to in the text as the Staatsoper, and the Komische Oper. The reader who wishes to explore the subject more fully – for there have been other changes of names down the years – should consult the entry on Berlin in the *Concise Oxford Dictionary of Opera*.

ABBADO, Claudio, b. 1933, Milan, Italy. Won the Koussevitsky Prize at Tanglewood (1958), then conducted in Italy, Germany and Austria. Mitropoulos Prize (1963). Debuts (1965) at La Scala, Milan, and in England with the Hallé. At Salzburg Festival (1965–). After being made Director of the Orchestra at La Scala (1968), he became Artistic Director (1971–79), and now as Chief Conductor, spends some six months at the great theatre

Despite Herculean labours at La Scala, Claudio Abbado enjoys a triumphant international career.

every year. Covent Garden and Metropolitan, New York, debuts with *Don Carlos* (1968). Became Principal Conductor, Vienna Philharmonic (1971), touring widely with the orchestra. Principal Conductor, London Symphony Orchestra (1979–): he made his London debut with the orchestra in 1966. As his awe-inspiring credits indicate, he is one of the most gifted conductors of the day. His operatic repertoire embraces Nono and Berg as well as the Italian classics. A renowned Verdian and Rossinian, he also has a very wide concert repertory, notably in Russian music. His 1977 *Carmen* at the Edinburgh Festival is already a legend, while at La Scala, he has successfully brought opera to new audiences of workers and young people. His 1980 triumphs included Schoenberg's *Erwartung* at La Scala.

ABRAVANEL, Maurice, b. 1903, Salonika, Greece. Berlin State Opera and Metropolitan Opera (1936–38), since when posts have included Musical Director, Balanchine Ballet Co. and Musical Director, Utah Symphony.

ACKERMANN, Otto, b. 1909, Bucharest, Rumania; d. Berne, Switzerland, 1960. Posts included Berne (1935–47), Cologne, where he was Generalmusikdirektor (1935–58) and Zurich (1958–60).

ADLER, Kurt, b. 1905, Vienna, Austria. Assistant Conductor to Toscanini at Salzburg (1936–37). Chicago Opera (1938–42), then went to San Francisco, first as conductor and chorus master (1943) of the Opera, then as General Director (1953–). The company has become very adventurous and most distinguished under his management.

ADLER, Peter, b. 1899, Jablonec, Czechoslovakia. After European posts, went to USA (1939). American debut with the New York Philharmonic (1940). Best known as Musical Director and Artistic Director/Conductor of NBC Opera Theater (1949–). American citizen.

AJMONE-MARSAN, Guido, b. Turin. A winner of a number of international prizes, in the 1970s he conducted many leading orchestras, including the London Symphony Orchestra, Chicago Symphony, Cleveland Orchestra, NDR Hamburg etc. Operatic debut, Spoleto, with *The Queen of Spades* (1976). Has also conducted opera in Britain, including *Bohème* for Welsh National Opera. Debut with Royal Philharmonic Orchestra and Hallé Orchestra (1977–78). City of Birmingham Symphony Orchestra (1979–80).

ALBRECHT, Gerd, b. 1935, Essen, Germany. Also pianist and violinist. Posts include Kassel, (1966–72), Chief Conductor, Deutsche Oper, Berlin (1972–) and Tonhalle, Zürich (1975–80) for concerts. He has conducted widely in Europe and elsewhere. Much praised for his conducting of Reimann's *Lear* at the Munich Festival (1978).

ALESSANDRO, Victor, b. 1915, Waco, Texas. Musical Director, Oklahoma

Symphony Orchestra (1938–51), after which he became Director of the San Antonio Symphony Orchestra and Grand Opera Festival (1950).

ALLDIS, John, b. 1929, London, England. Founder/Conductor of the John Alldis Choir in 1962 (to specialize in new music). Founder/Conductor, London Symphony Chorus (1966). Conductor, London Philharmonic Choir (1969–). Other posts include Conductor, Groupe Vocal de France, Paris (1979–) and Guest Conductor, Suddeutsche Rundfunk. A renowned choral conductor.

ALLERS, Franz, b. 1905, Carlsbad, Czechoslovakia. He has worked widely in Europe and America. Metropolitan Opera, New York (1963–). Has conducted leading European and American symphony orchestras. Generalmusikdirektor, Munich Staatstheater am Gaertnerplatz (1973).

ALMEIDA, Antonio de, b. 1928, Paris, France. Radio Portugal Orchestra (1957–60). Director, Stuttgart Philharmonic Orchestra (1960–64), since when he has conducted many leading European and American orchestras and visited Japan.

ALMGREN, Tore, b. 1935, Stockholm, Sweden. Also a pianist and composer. A leading Swedish conductor, he has also performed in Germany and Britain.

ALTANI, Ippolit, b. 1846, Ukraine; d. Moscow, 1919. Kiev Opera (1867–82). Chief Conductor, Bolshoi, Moscow (1882–1906), conducting first Moscow

Boris (1888), Queen of Spades (1891) and other premières.

ALWYN, Kenneth, b. 1928, London, England. Also composer. Associate Conductor, Sadler's Wells Theatre Ballet (1952–56). Royal Ballet (1956–59). Conducted TV programmes. Principal Conductor, BBC Northern Ireland Orchestra (until 1975). A regular broadcaster.

AMADUCCI, Bruno, b. 1925, Lugano-Viganello, Switzerland. Metropolitan New York, Paris Opera, Vienna State Opera etc.

ANDERSEN, Karsten, b. 1920, Oslo, Norway. Musical Director, Stavanger (1945–64). Chief Conductor, Iceland Symphony Orchestra (1973–). Has conducted in most European countries and in America.

ANGERER, Paul, b. 1927, Vienna, Austria. Also composer, violist and harpsichordist. Posts include Musical Director, Ulm (1966–68), Opera Director, Salzburger Landestheater (1967–72). Musical Director, SW German Chamber Orchestra (1970–), Artistic Director Hellbruner Spiele (1970–71).

ANNOVAZZI, Napoleone, b. 1907, Florence, Italy. Also composer. Has conducted at most leading European operas houses. Founder and Conductor, Chamber Orchestra of Barcelona (1946–48). Artistic Director, Dublin Grand Opera Society.

ANSERMET, Ernest, b. 1883, Vevey, Switzerland; d. Geneva, 1969. Also author of books on music and philosophy. First a professor of mathematics, making his conducting debut in 1911. With Ballets Russes (1915), giving premières of Stravinsky's *L'Histoire du Soldat* (1918), *Renard* (1922) and *Les Noces* (1923), also Falla's *Le Tricorne*, Ravel's *La Valse* and Satie's *Parade*. Conductor of L'Orchestre de la Suisse Romande (1918–67), which he founded. Renowned for his Debussy, Ravel and Stravinsky, also for his *Boris Godunov* and *Die Zauberflöte*.

ANTONICELLI, Giuseppe, b. 1896, Cozenza, Italy; d. Trieste, 1980. Debut, Turin (1923), becoming a leading conductor at La Scala etc. Particularly associated with Teatro Verdi, Trieste as General Administrator (1937–45; 1950–66).

ARMSTRONG, Richard, b. 1943, Leicester, England. With Welsh National Opera (1968–), becoming the very successful Musical Director (1973–). Notable successes in modern opera and Janacek.

ARNOLD, John, b. 1944, London, England. Debut with Royal Ballet (1968), since when he has conducted leading British and European orchestras.

ARNOLD, Malcolm, b. 1921, Northampton, England. Originally a trumpeter, he has conducted since 1948, though best known as a successful composer.

ASHKENAZY, Vladimir, b. 1937, Gorky, USSR. One of the world's great pianists, he is turning more and more

to conducting as well, notably with the Philharmonia (1976–). He conducted them (and also played) on a tour of Austria and Germany in late 1979.

ATHERTON, David, b. 1944, Blackpool, England. After notable successes as an opera conductor at Cambridge, he joined the staff of the Royal Opera, Covent Garden (1967), becoming the youngest conductor to appear with the Company (1968). He has since conducted more than 100 performances there. Founded London Sinfonietta (1967) and was Musical Director (until 1973), giving many contemporary works. Youngest Proms conductor (1968), since when he has conducted widely abroad. Artistic Director and conductor of the Stravinsky Festival (1979–), presenting all the composer's works. Principal Conductor, Royal Liverpool Philharmonic Orchestra.

ATLAS, Dalia, b. Haifa, Israel. Permanent Conductor and Director, Haifa Chamber Orchestra (1963–). Guest Conductor, Royal Liverpool Philharmonic Orchestra (1964–65), since when she had conducted Haifa Symphony Orchestra, Houston Symphony Orchestra etc. Conductor, Israel Pro Musica Orchestra.

ATZMON, Moshe, b. 1931, Budapest, Hungary. Chief Conductor, Sydney Symphony Orchestra (1969–72). Chief Conductor, NDR Orchestra, Hamburg (1972–78), and has conducted British orchestras, the Vienna Philharmonic Orchestra etc.

AUERBACH, Cynthia, b. 1940, Spring Valley, New York USA. Also stage director of operas. Founder, Stage Director and Conductor, Manhattan School of Music Children's Opera Theatre (1967–   ).

B

BAGIN, Pavol, b. 1933, Kosice, Czechoslovakia. Artistic Principal and Conductor of the Opera of the Slovak National Theatre, Bratislava (1971–), and has conducted widely in Eastern Europe.

BAHNER, Gert, b. 1930, Neuweise/ Erzgebirge, Germany. Komische Oper, Berlin (1954–58: 1965–74) etc. Chief Conductor, Leipzig Opera (1974–) where he conducted a notable Ring (1976). Conducted the Company in Cardiff and Birmingham (1980).

BALKWILL, Bryan, b. 1922, London, England. Associate Conductor, Glyndebourne (1953–59). Resident Conductor, Royal Opera House, Covent Garden (1959–65). Musical Director, Sadler's Wells Opera (1966–69), and has conducted widely in Britain and abroad.

BALL, Christopher, b. 1936, Leeds, England. Also clarinettist and composer. Has conducted Royal Ballet, City of Birmingham Symphony Orchestra, the BBC Northern Symphony Orchestra, BBC Scottish Orchestra and at Covent Garden.

BALLING, Michael, b. 1866, Heidingsfeld, Germany; d. Darmstadt, 1925. Assistant at Bayreuth (1896). Bayreuth (1904–25), also conducted *Ring* in English (Edinburgh, 1910). With the Hallé (1912–14), where he succeeded Richter. His nationality lost him his job when war broke out, which was Manchester's ill-fortune.

BAMBERGER, Carl, b. 1902, Vienna, Austria. With German opera houses (1924–31). A wide-ranging guest conductor, he has held various posts in North America. Wrote *The Conductor's Art* (1965).

BARANOVÍC, Krešimir, b. 1894, Sibenik, (now) Yugoslavia; d. Belgrade, 1975. Also composer. Music Director at Zagreb (1915–25), Belgrade (1927–29) and Bratislava (1945–46) operas, greatly extending the repertoires of each.

BARBIER, Guy, b. 1924, Namur, Belgium. Also composer. Since his debut in 1957, he has conducted widely at home and abroad: concerts, opera and ballet. Director of the Royal Conservatoire of Music, Liège; and Founder and Director, Orchestre Mozart de Bruxelles.

Sir John Barbirolli was dubbed 'Glorious John' by Vaughan Williams. Not only Mancunians agree with him.

BARBIROLLI, (Sir) John, b. 1899, London, England; d. London, 1970. Of Italian parentage, he began as a cellist, making his debut aged eleven. Formed chamber orchestra (1924), British National Opera Co. (1926), Royal Opera House, Covent Garden (1928), becoming Musical Director of its English Company (1930), and conducting there till 1933, then again in 1937. Meanwhile, he was Permanent Conductor of the BBC Scottish Orchestra and the Leeds Symphony Orchestra, also conducting the Hallé etc. Succeeded Toscanini with the New York Philharmonic (1936–43), an invidious task which he survived with some honour. Returned to the Hallé (1943), remaining with them for twenty-four seasons of glorious achievement. Houston Symphony Orchestra (1961–67). At Covent Garden again in the early '50s, he was then absent from opera, except in concert form until he conducted a Rome *Aida* just before his death.

Barbirolli had suffered from ill-health for many years. He was the only British conductor of his day apart from Beecham to have an international reputation. He excelled in Romantic music, satisfied the exacting Alma Mahler with his interpretations of her husband's works, and was a champion of Vaughan Williams, who fulsomely but understandably dubbed him 'Glorious John'. Yet his greatest achievement for many was his rebuilding of the Hallé, a 'skeleton of a Hallé orchestra, war-denuded,' as Neville Cardus called it, when he rejoined it in the middle of the war. In Manchester – and elsewhere – he was greatly loved, as a man as well as a conductor. Knighted in 1949.

BARENBOIM, Daniel, b. 1942, Buenos Aires. Made his debut as a pianist in Buenos Aires, aged seven. A regular concert pianist in Europe and the USA from the mid '50s, he became a noted conductor as well and has conducted or been a soloist with most leading orchestras. Associated with Brighton Festival (1967–), also with the Edinburgh Festival, where he has conducted opera: he is a notable interpreter of Mozart's operas and, very differently of *Samson et Dalila* (Orange 1978). He is also Artistic Director of the Orchestre de Paris.

BARKER, John, b. 1931, Twickenham,

England. Head of Music Staff and Chorus Master, Royal Opera, Covent Garden (1975–), having previously worked at Glyndebourne and Sadler's Wells/English National Opera. Has conducted over 600 performances of opera, also the New Philharmonic and the Orquesta Sinfonica Nacional of Mexico.

BARSHAI, Rudolph, b. 1924, Labinskaya, USSR. Founder of the Moscow Chamber Orchestra (1955).

BARTOLETTI, Bruno, b. 1926, Sesto Fiorentino, Italy. Debut, Florence (*Rigoletto*, 1953), since when he has established himself as a leading opera conductor. Chicago Opera (1957–). Rome Opera (1965–71).

BARZIN, Leon, b. 1900, Brussels, Belgium. Musical Director, National Orchestral Association (1930–57: 1969–76). Hartford Symphony Orchestra (1940–45). New York City Ballet (1948–58) and guest appearance in many countries.

BASIC, Mladen, b. 1917, Yugoslavia. Chief Conductor, Mozarteum Orchestra and Opera House, Salzburg (1959–68). Other posts include Zagreb Philharmonic Orchestra (1970–76) and Generalmusikdirektor, Mainz (1976–). Very wide repertoire.

BAUDO, Serge, b. 1927, Marseilles. French conductor and composer. Co-founder (with Charles Munch) of the Orchestre de Paris, which he conducted until 1970. Conducts operas also. Principal Conductor, Orchestre Philharmonique de Lyon.

BAUMGARTNER, Rudolf, b. 1917, Zurich, Switzerland. Co-founder, the Lucerne Strings, also Artistic Director, Lucerne International Festival of Music. A distinguished scholar-conductor.

BEAUDRY, Jacques, b. 1929, Sorel, Quebec, Canada. As well as conducting in Montreal, he has appeared at the Paris Opéra and Opéra-Comique also at the Metropolitan, New York (1967–) and in many parts of Europe.

BECKETT, Sibthorpe, b. 1920, Kingston, Jamaica. A leading figure in Jamaican music. Founded Jamaica Philharmonic Orchestra (1940), becoming Resident Conductor and Director of Music.

BEDFORD, Steuart, b. 1939, London, England. Artistic Director, Aldeburgh Festival (1974). Artistic Director, English Opera Group, which became English Music Theatre (1976–). Has also conducted at Covent Garden, Metropolitan New York, in Europe, Canada etc.

BEECHAM, (Sir) Thomas, b. 1879, St. Helens, England; d. London, 1961. Arguably the greatest, certainly the best known and most controversial of British conductors. His influence on music and opera in Britain was colossal, while his fame abroad, most notably in America, was immense. Most orchestral players adored him;

many, though not all singers, had less reason to love him. He was a great wit and a man of widespread culture who enjoyed life to the full. Consequently, he was underrated by some as a dilettante or worse. Yet he was both totally professional (bar lapses) and amateur in the true sense of the word.

The son of Joseph Beecham of pills fame (money from which was to be put to magnificent use), his musical education was informal. Conducted a touring opera company (1902–04). Gave his first concerts (1905). Founded the New Symphony Orchestra (1906) and Beecham Symphony Orchestra (1909). Beecham's first opera season (Covent Garden, 1910) is legendary, although he was still learning. It included the first English *Elektra*, Ethel Smyth's *The Wreckers* and Delius's *A Village Romeo and Juliet*. By 1914, he had given the English premières of *Salome*, *Ariadne au Naxos* (first version) and *Rosenkavalier*, presented fabulous seasons of Russian opera (1913–14), including Chaliapin, and the even more historic Diaghilev ballet season of 1911. He also toured opera outside London. By 1920, when financial disaster overtook him, he had helped save the Hallé, the London Symphony Orchestra and the Royal Philharmonic Society, and given opera seasons with

Inspirational, witty, wide-ranging, impish and supremely talented, Sir Thomas Beecham was unique.

the very strong Beecham Opera Company in London and Manchester, which are remembered with joy and with awe.

By 1924, he was able to resume operations, slowly at first. 1932 was a great year: he founded the London Philharmonic Orchestra and returned to Covent Garden as Chief Conductor and Artistic Director (1932–39). He took the London Philharmonic to Germany (1936) and gave four *Rings* at Covent Garden (1934/'35/'36/'39). In the USA (1941–44), he conducted at the Metropolitan, New York and, as Harold Schonberg has written, 'every orchestra in sight.' Back in Britain, he founded the Royal Philharmonic Orchestra (1946). To the distress of many and relief of other weaker spirits, he was not asked to return to Covent Garden to master-mind the creation of the new company, though he later gave memorable performances of *Meistersinger* and a season of *The Bohemian Girl*. He conducted the original version of *Ariadne auf Naxos* at the Edinburgh Festival (1950) and a handful of other operas before a final spell at the Colon, Buenos Aires (1958). And all the while his concerts with the Royal Philharmonic were always events and often magical occasions.

Beecham was at his commanding best in Mozart, Haydn, Berlioz, Delius (whose supreme advocate he was), Strauss, Handel, Bizet, Schubert ... it is a long list; yet he could illuminate Wagner, Beethoven and other composers not particularly congenial to him.

Authenticity did not bother him when it came to certain composers. His *Messiah* had the purists hopping –

he said that a musicologist is a person who can read music but cannot hear it – while his Mozartian orchestra was large. Yet there are many alive who swear he was the supreme Mozartian of his day. He was a great improviser, believing in spontaneity and varying his interpretations, even from rehearsal to performance. With his own players the results were exhilarating in the extreme, not least for them. Knighted in 1916 before inheriting his father's baronetcy, he became a British Institution. As when Garrick died, Beecham's death eclipsed the gaiety of nations.

BEETHOVEN, Ludwig van, b. 1770, Bonn, Germany; d. Vienna, 1827. As noted in Chapter 1, the great composer was also a conductor, though his increasing deafness finally made him a disastrous one. He was one of the pioneers of modern conducting, though a cruel fate prevented great achievements as a conductor.

BEHR, Jan, b. 1911, Krnov, Czechoslovakia. Debut: with *La Traviata* at the German Opera House, Prague (1936). At the Metropolitan, New York (1951–) Cinncinnati Opera etc.

BEINUM, Eduard van, b. 1901 Arnhem, Holland; d. Amsterdam, 1959. Became Mengelberg's assistant with the Concertgebouw, Amsterdam (1932), succeeding him (1938–58). Conducted London Philharmonic Orchestra, Los Angeles Symphony Orchestra etc. Died before reaching the heights to which he seemed destined.

BELLEZZA, Vincenzo, b. 1888, Bitonto, Italy; d. Rome, 1964. Debut, Naples (1908). After making his name in Italy, conducted at Teatro Colon, Buenos Aires, then at Metropolitan Opera, New York (1926–35) and Royal Opera House, Covent Garden (1926–30: 1935–36) including Melba's legendary Farewell (1926). Rome and other Italian houses (1935–64). At the London Stoll Theatre (1957) and Drury Lane (1958) with Italian companies.

BELLUGI, Piero, b. 1924, Florence, Italy. After his debut at La Scala, Milan (1960), posts have included Permanent Conductor, Radio Symphony Orchestra, Turin (1969–).

BENIC, Vladimir, b. 1922, Zagreb, Yugoslavia. Has conducted widely at home and abroad. Musical Director, Rijeka Opera and Symphony Orchestra. Opatija Opera Festival (1963–69). Was Conductor, Zagreb Philharmonic Orchestra. Has conducted widely outside Yugoslavia.

BENSTORP, Lars, b. 1938, Jönköping, Sweden. A leading Swedish conductor, whose debut was with the Norrköping Symphony Orchestra (1963).

BENTLEY, Keith, b. 1946, Middlesbrough, England. Conductor of opera in the North of England, including Cleveland Opera.

BENZI, Roberto, b. 1937, Marseilles, France. Also a composer. A child prodigy, he made his debut in Bayonne (1948). Musical Director, Orchestra of Bordeaux-Aquitaine (1973) and has been a guest conductor in many countries.

BERGEL, Erich, b. 1930, Rosenan, Romania. Chief Conductor, State Philharmonic Orchestra of Cluj (1959–71), becoming a resident of West Germany in 1972. Since then, he has conducted widely in Europe, the Americas and Japan. He made his US debut with the Houston Symphony Orchestra (1975), where he is now Principal Guest Conductor. He has conducted most leading British orchestras, the Berlin Philharmonic etc., and is particularly well known for his Bruckner and his masterly analysis of Bach's *The Art of Fugue*.

BERGLUND, Paavo, b. 1929, Helsinki, Finland. Assistant Conductor, Finnish Radio Symphony Orchestra (1956–62), Principal Conductor (1962–71). Gave a series of Sibelius concerts with the Bournemouth Symphony Orchestra (1965), becoming its Principal Conductor (1972–79). Principal Conductor, Helsinki Philharmonic Orchestra (1975–79).

BERLIOZ, Hector, b. 1803, La Côte-St. André, France; d. Paris, 1869. France's greatest composer was the first great modern French conductor. As noted in the previous and following chapters, he ranks as one of the handful of founding fathers of modern conducting. In his case it was partly to avoid his own music being butchered. He also conducted other music in Europe and England, and was widely admired by his contemporaries.

BERNARDI, Mario, b. 1930, Kirkland Lake, Ontario, Canada. Musical Director, Sadler's Wells Opera (1966–69). National Arts Centre, Ottawa (1969–82). Guest conductor of opera and concerts, including Chicago Symphony Orchestra, San Francisco Opera etc.

BERNIER, Francoys, b. 1927, Quebec, Canada. Musical Director, Montreal Festival (1956–59). General Director, Quebec Symphony Orchestra (1959–69). Founded Dept. of Music, University of Ottawa (1969). Has conducted widely in Canada and France.

BERNSTEIN, Leonard, b. 1918, Lawrence, Massachusetts, USA. Also composer, pianist, educator. This internationally famous latterday Renaissance Man was the first native-born American conductor to 'make it', for before him only foreigners had been musical directors of major American orchestras. Controversial, especially in the early years after his breakthrough, he remains a phenomenon whose career and personality have publicized music to splendid effect.

Koussevitsky's assistant at the Berkshire Music Center, Tanglewood (1942), becoming Rodzinski's assistant conductor with the New York Philharmonic (1943). When Bruno Walter fell ill, Rodzinski insisted that Bernstein take his place (November 14, 1943), from which moment the Bernstein legend was born. So rocket-like was his rise to fame that, the public apart, his detractors were legion. They are not totally dead to this day. At the Berkshire Music Center (1948–55), where he had given the first US *Peter Grimes* (1946). New York City Center Orchestra (1945–48), then guest conducting (and the delightful *Candide*). New York Philharmonic (1958–), as co-Conductor, becoming Laureate Conductor for Life (1969). He had taken over the orchestra which was low in morale and discipline, rapidly transforming it. A number of notable operatic performances at La Scala, the Metropolitan and elsewhere, including a famous *Falstaff* at the Vienna State Opera (1966). Of the handful of conductors who can lecture to adults and young people successfully, he is the finest.

Leonard Bernstein, latter day Renaissance Man and the first native American conductor to 'make it.'

BERTINI, Gary, b. 1927, Birzewo, Bessarabia. Also composer. Debut with Israel Philharmonic Orchestra (1955), since when he has conducted in Europe and America. Founder and Musical Director, Israel Chamber Orchestra (1965). Currently Artistic Director, Jerusalem Symphony Orchestra.

BERTON, Pierre-Montan, b. 1727, Maubert-Fontaines, France; d. Paris, 1780. Conductor at Paris Opéra (1755–78), where he greatly improved orchestral standards. Also a bass and composer.

BEVIGNANI, Enrico, b. 1841, Naples; d. Naples, 1903. Also composer. Covent Garden (1869–87: 1890–96), conducting first London *Aida* (1876) *Gioconda* (1883) and *Pagliacci* (1893). Metropolitan, New York (1894–1900), also in St. Petersburg and Moscow.

BISHOP, (Sir) Henry, b. 1786, London; d. London, 1855. Also composer. A specialist in 'improving' masterpieces, notably in his reign as Musical Director, Covent Garden (1810–24), where he rewrote parts of *Figaro*, *Fidelio*, *Don Giovanni* and *Barbiere* etc., including gems of his own. He was not the only one to do this. Knighted in 1842.

BLECH, Harry, b. 1916, London, England. Founder and Leader of Blech String Quartet (1933–50). Founder and Conductor, London Wind Players (1942). Founder and Conductor, London Mozart Players (1949–) also Founder and Musical Director, Haydn-Mozart Society. His concerts have always been enormously popular.

BLECH, Leo, b. 1871, Aachen, Germany; d. Berlin, 1958. Also composer. Best known as an operatic conductor: Aachen (1893–99). Deutsches Theater, Prague (1899–1906). Berlin Royal Opera (1906–23) becoming General-musikdirektor (1913). American tour with Vienna State Opera ensemble (1923). Jointly in charge of Berlin State Opera with Kleiber, but forced to leave (1937), being Jewish. Riga (1937–41), Stockholm (1941–47). Berlin Städtische Oper (1949–54). A famous Wagnerian.

BODANSKY, Artur, b. 1877, Vienna; d. New York, 1939. Mahler's assistant at the Vienna Opera (1902–04), then at Prague, Mannheim and Covent Garden, where he conducted the first English *Parsifal* (1914). Metropolitan, New York (1915–39, except for 1928–29 season). His notorious 'Bodansky cuts' infuriated local Wagnerians.

BÖHM, Karl, b. 1894, Graz, Austria. Originally trained for the law, this doyen of Austro-German conductors started at Graz (1917–21), becoming Principal Conductor (1920). Karl Muck recommended him to Bruno Walter at Munich (1921–27). General-musikdirektor, Darmstadt (1927–31), then Hamburg (1931–33). Dresden State Opera (1934–43), where he became a famous interpreter of Richard Strauss, who dedicated *Daphne* and *Die schweigsame Frau* to him: he gave the premières of both. Vienna State Opera (1943–45), returning to open the new house as General-musikdirektor (1954). He resigned (1955) after criticisms of his absences abroad. Has conducted Vienna Philharmonic Orchestra (1933–), Berlin Philharmonic, New York Philharmonic, London Symphony Orchestra and at the Metropolitan, New York (1957–). Covent Garden (1936: 1977–79). Regularly at Salzburg and leading Italian theatres, also at Bayreuth (1962–70). As famous for his Mozart performances as for his Richard Strauss, indeed he is now (1980) the doyen of Mozart conductors. Using a small baton, and with gestures at a bare minimum, he controls his forces in his Olympian old age with his piercing eyes.

BONYNGE, Richard, b. 1930, Sydney, Australia. Also pianist. Concert debut, Santa Cecilia Orchestra, Rome (1962). Opera debut, *Faust* (Vancouver, 1963), since when he has conducted at Covent Garden (1964–). Metropolitan, New York (1970–) and many other opera houses. Specializes in *bel canto* works and the French repertoire. The husband of Joan Sutherland, it was he who guided her to her true repertoire and, with Tullio Serafin and others, to international fame. Musical Director, Australian Opera (1975–).

BOSKOVSKY, Willi, b. 1909, Vienna. The world famous conductor of the New Year concerts of the Vienna Philharmonic Orchestra (1954–), as well as its Leader and the founder of the Vienna Octet etc. A renowned expert of operetta and its traditions, and equally renowned for his mastery of the Viennese waltz.

BOULEZ, Pierre, b. 1925, Montbrison, France. This famous composer is also a notable conductor, renowned for his Wagner, Debussy and Berg. Despite his polemical wish to blow up all opera houses, he is often to be found in them, though never conducting Italian opera. Musical Director, New York Philharmonic (1971–77). Chief Conductor, BBC Symphony Orchestra (1971–75). In charge of the centenary *Ring* at Bayreuth (1976), where he first conducted in 1966.

BOULT, (Sir) Adrian, b. 1889, Chester, England. The doyen of British conductors, unflamboyant in manner, spectacular in decades of achievement. Highlights of a very long career even by conductors' standards include Musical Director, City of Birmingham Symphony Orchestra (1924–30); Director of Music, BBC, (1930–42: 1959–60); Conductor, BBC Symphony Orchestra (1930–50); and Chief Conductor of London Philharmonic Orchestra (1950–57), becoming its President (1966). Conducted the Bach Choir (1928–33) and was a popular and, in his final performances, an adored figure at the Proms. His repertoire is immense, but his chief fame is as a conductor of Elgar, Holst, Vaughan Williams and other English composers. Knighted in 1937.

BRADSHAW, Richard, b. 1944, Rugby, England. Director, New London Ensemble and Choir (1972–). Saltarello Choir (1972–75). Many guest appearances at home and abroad.

BRAEM, Thuring, b. 1944, Basel, Switzerland. Also composer. A leading Swiss conductor, whose posts include

Conservatoire Orchestra, Basel (1973).

BRAITHWAITE, Nicholas, b. 1939, London, England. Son of Warwick Braithwaite (below). Associate Conductor, Bournemouth Symphony Orchestra (1967–70). Associate Principal Conductor, Sadler's Wells Opera (1971–74). Guest appearances with many orchestras. Director of Glyndebourne Touring Opera (1977–). Director, Norwegian Radio Orchestra (1977–).

BRAITHWAITE, Warwick, b. 1898, Dunedin, New Zealand; d. London, 1971. O'Mara Opera Co. (1919–22), then joined British National Opera Co. Musical Director, BBC, Cardiff and Conductor of National Orchestra of Wales, then at Sadler's Wells Opera (1933–40). Covent Garden (1950–52). Australian Opera (1954). Musical Director, Welsh National Opera (1956–60). Sadler's Wells Opera (1960–68). As this summary suggests, he played a notable part in the growth of opera in Britain.

BRANDT, Michel, b. 1934, Rennes, France. Staedtebund Theater, Biel-Solothurn (1961–64). Cologne Opera (1964–71), becoming Senior Lecturer, Royal Northern College of Music, Manchester (1973). Many guest appearances in Europe, Israel and USA.

BRITTEN, (Lord) Benjamin, b. 1913, Lowestoft, England; d. Aldeburgh, 1976. Britain's greatest composer was a very fine conductor, not only of his own works, at Aldeburgh and elsewhere.

BROTT, Boris, b. 1944, Montreal, Canada. Assistant Conductor, Toronto Symphony Orchestra (1963–65). Principal Conductor, Northern Sinfonia (1964–68). Assistant Conductor, New York Philharmonic (1968–69). Other posts include CBC Winnipeg Orchestra (1975–). Has conducted widely as a guest artist.

BROWN, Iona, b. 1941, Salisbury. Director of Academy of St. Martin-in-the-Fields from Leader's desk, and regular director of Academy's Chamber Group.

BRYDON, Roderick, b. 1939, Edinburgh, Scotland. A leading young operatic conductor, notably with Scottish Opera and, since 1964, with Sadler's Wells/English National Opera. Artistic Director, Scottish Chamber Orchestra. Has conducted widely in Germany, including *Albert Herring*: he is a noted conductor of Britten. *Così fan tutte* in Bordeaux (1979). He has also conducted the Scottish National Orchestra and Munich Philharmonic Orchestra.

BUCKLEY, Emerson, b. 1916, New York City, USA. His many American posts include New York City Opera Co. (1955–67), Central City Opera Festival (1956–69), and regular seasons in Miami, Baltimore and Seattle. Much radio work.

BUGAJ, Tomasz, b. 1950, Warsaw, Poland. Regularly conducts Warsaw Chamber Orchestra. Radio Symphony Orchestra, Cracow (1977–). International Conductors Award in

Britain (1978), the prize including 40 concerts with the Bournemouth Symphony Orchestra.

BUKETOFF, Igor, b. 1915, Hartford, Conn., USA. Fort Wayne Philharmonic Orchestra (1948–66). Regular guest appearances at home and abroad. Musical Director, Iceland State Symphony (1964–65). Founder/ Chairman, World Music Bank (1957–). Artistic Director, St. Paul Opera Association (1968–).

BÜLOW, Hans von, b. 1830, Dresden, Germany; d. Cairo, 1894. Also a great pianist. This first virtuoso conductor (see Chapter 1) was trained for music, then the law. But the first *Lohengrin* (Weimar, 1850) so overwhelmed him that he returned to music, studied with Wagner at Zürich, then the piano with

Hans von Bülow, the first virtuoso conductor, was autocratic and difficult, but undoubtedly great.

Liszt, whose daughter Cosima he married. Chief Conductor, Royal Opera, Munich (1864–69), giving the first *Tristan und Isolde* (1965) and *Meistersinger* (1868). When his wife left him for Wagner, he toured Europe, mainly as a pianist, concentrating on conducting from 1878, when he became Conductor of the Court Theatre, Hanover. In charge of the great Meiningen Orchestra (1880–85). This was ideal for him for, according to Weingartner, when conducting opera, he concentrated almost entirely on the orchestra, 'as if it was a symphonic work.' Autocratic, difficult and often ferociously rude, and finally suffering from depression and mental breakdown, his greatness was beyond doubt, as noted by his young assistant, Richard Strauss. He became a champion of Brahms. From 1885, he made guest appearances throughout Europe, playing little but German music. He had publicly insulted Italian music in Milan (1874), but made amends to Verdi at least by later taking back what he had first said about his *Requiem*. From 1885, he regularly conducted the Berlin Philharmonic Orchestra.

BURGOS, See FRUHBECK de BURGOS.

BUSCH, Fritz, b. Siegen, Germany, 1890; d. London, 1951. One of the great opera conductors of the century and, with Carl Ebert, the artistic creator of the Glyndebourne Opera. After posts at Riga (1909) and Aachen (1912), he became Generalmusik-direktor of Stuttgart (1918), going on to Dresden (1922–33) and presiding over one of its most splendid periods. An opponent of Hitler (Aryan, not Jewish), he left Germany, first for the Teatro Colon, Buenos Aires (1933–36: 1941–45), then to Glyndebourne (1934). Conducted at each now legendary pre-war season and again in 1950 and 1951. At the Metropolitan, New York (1945–49). He also made guest appearances in Europe and America. Apart from his genius for creating an ensemble, especially at Dresden and Glyndebourne, he was a great Mozartian and renowned for his Verdi as well as his Wagner.

C

CADUFF, Sylvia, b. 1938, Chur, Switzerland. A pupil of von Karajan, she is currently (1980–) West Germany's first female Generalmusik-direktor at Solingen. She has also conducted the Berlin Philharmonic, the Royal Philharmonic etc.

CALDWELL, Sarah, b. 1928, Maryville, Missouri, USA. Also a producer. Founder of Boston Opera Company (1957–), which she has directed with flair amounting to genius. Her policy has been adventurous, conducting her own productions, which have included the USA's first *Les Troyens*, *Moses und Aron* and *War and Peace*. She has also conducted the New York City Opera (1973) and became the first woman conductor at the New York Metropolitan Opera (1976).

CAMERON, Basil, b. 1885, Reading, England; d. 1975. After conducting municipal orchestras (Torquay, Hastings, Harrogate), he appeared with leading London orchestras from the 1930s, also with the San Francisco Orchestra (1930–32) and Seattle Symphony Orchestra (1932–38). For many years associated with the Proms.

CAMPANINI, Cleofonte, b. 1860, Parma, Italy; d. Chicago, 1919. Metropolitan Opera, New York (1883–84), after which his posts included La Scala, Milan (1903–06) and Covent Garden (1904–12). His London premières included *Madama Butterfly* (1905). Artistic Director, Manhattan Opera (1906–09). Chicago Opera (1910–19), becoming General Manager (1918–19). One of the finest operatic conductors of his time, his La Scala premières included *Adriana Lecouvreur*, *Madama Butterfly* – that ill-fated first performance – and Giordano's *Siberia*.

CANTELLI, Guido, b. 1920, Novara, Italy; d. in an air crash, 1956. Destined, it seemed, to be Toscanini's successor, he died just after becoming Director of La Scala, Milan. Remembered as a brilliant symphonic conductor. Notable performances with the Philharmonia and the Boston Symphony.

CAPUANA, Franco, b. 1894, Fano, Italy; d. Naples, 1969. La Scala (1937–40: 1946–52), becoming Musical Director in 1949. Many appearances elsewhere, including Covent Garden, where he conducted the first opera after the war, *La Traviata* with the San

Carlo Co. (1946). As well as the Italian repertory, he gave notable Wagner and Richard Strauss performances. Died while conducting *Mosè* at the San Carlo on the opening night of the 1969–70 season.

CAREWE, John, b. 1933, Derby, England. BBC Welsh Orchestra (1966–71). Principal Conductor, Brighton Philharmonic Orchestra (1974–). Founded the New Music Ensemble (1957) and is a notable conductor of modern music.

CARIDIS, Militiades, b. 1923, Danzig, Poland. Posts include Artistic and Musical Director, Philharmonic Society, Oslo (1969–75) and Conductor-in-Chief, Duisburg Symphony Orchestra (1975–).

CASADESUS, Jean-Claude, b. France. A leading young French conductor. Debut at Paris Opéra (1969), since when his posts have included Musical Director, Orchestre Philharmonique de Lille (1976–). Has conducted in many European countries. Invited by Barenboim to take over the direction of the Youth Orchestra of the Orchestre de Paris (1979–).

CASALS, Pablo, b. 1876, Vendrell, Spain; d. San Juan, Puerto Rico, 1973. The great cellist was also a composer and conductor of note, including of his own orchestra, founded in Barcelona in 1920.

CECCATO, Aldo, b. 1934, Milan, Italy. Musical Director and Conductor, Detroit Symphony Orchestra (1973–76) and a regular guest conductor in Europe and America, including Glyndebourne, Covent Garden, New York Philharmonic, Cleveland Orchestra and Chicago Symphony.

CELIBIDACHE, Sergiu, b. 1912, Romania. Chief Conductor, Berlin Philharmonic Orchestra (1945–51). He has made guest appearances in North and South America, Britain and Europe, including regular appearances with the London Symphony Orchestra (from 1978) after a long absence from Britain. Widely acclaimed for his performances of the classics, he is something of a legend in his own lifetime, not least because he does not make records or appear on television, and shuns publicity. He has done much research into the aesthetics and psychology of music.

On his return to London after two decades it took a little time for the public to rediscover him – there were none of his records in the current catalogue. Word of his prowess rapidly spread, while orchestras were prepared to give him extra rehearsals, so highly is he rated by his players.

CELIS, Fritz, b. 1929, Antwerp, Belgium. Also harpist and composer. Musical Director, and First Conductor, Royal Flemish Opera, and a guest conductor with many European orchestras.

CHAILLY, Riccardo, b. 1953, Milan, Italy, the son of the composer and administrator, Luciano Chailly. Has conducted widely in Italy. La Scala debut in *I Masnadieri* (1978), and has also conducted at Covent Garden, Chicago Opera etc. A very successful

German debut (1979) at Stuttgart with *Rigoletto*, and equally notable Proms debut (1980).

CHAPPLE, Stanley, b. 1900, London, England. Many guest appearances in Europe and USA. Director, Symphony Orchestra and Opera, University of Washington (1948–71).

CHARRY, Michael, b. 1933, New York City, USA. After various US posts, Assistant Conductor, Cleveland Orchestra (1965–72). Many guest performances in US, Europe, Mexico etc.

CHAVEZ, Carlos, b. 1899, Mexico City. Also composer. Founder/ Conductor, New Music Concerts, Mexico City (1923–25), since when he has played a leading role in Mexican music, including founding the National Symphony Orchestra. Has also conducted in North and South America (1935–).

CILLARIO, Carlo Felice, b. 1915, San Raphael, Argentina. Founder of Orchestra di Camera, Bologna (1946). Founder of Symphony Orchestra of Tucuman, Argentina (1948). Resident Conductor, Orchestra Sinfonica del Estado, Buenos Aires, then Resident Conductor, Angelicum of Milan. Conducted the legendary Callas, Gobbi, Zeffirelli *Tosca* at Covent Garden (1964) and has conducted at La Scala, Metropolitan etc. Notable success with Australian Opera as Musical Director (1969–71), then as a regular visitor (1975–).

CLEOBURY, Nicholas, b. 1950. Also organist and harpsichordist. Conductor, Schola Cantorum, Oxford (1973–) and has conducted other choirs, orchestras and operas. Conductor and Director, Bach Festival Choir. Chorus Director, London Choral Society.

CLEVA, Fausto, b. 1902, Trieste; d. Athens, 1971. Assistant Conductor Metropolitan, New York (1920–21), becoming Chorus Master (1935–42) and Head of the Italian repertory (1950). Artistic Director, Chicago Opera (1944–46). Also at San Francisco Opera, Cincinnati Summer Opera, Stockholm etc. Died in gloriously dramatic circumstances, conducting Gluck's *Orfeo* in the Theatre of Herodes Atticus adjoining the Acropolis.

CLUTYENS, André, b. 1905, Antwerp, Belgium; d. Paris, 1967. Antwerp Opera (1927–32) where his father had been a conductor. Toulouse, Bordeaux, Lyons, then with Paris Opéra and Opéra-Comique (1947–67), Bayreuth (1955–58; 1965), with regular appearances in Italy and Vienna.

COATES, Albert, b. 1882, St. Petersburg; d. Cape Town, 1953. Also a composer. This Anglo-Russian conductor began his career in Germany, his posts including Dresden (1908) and Mannheim (1910). Chief Conductor and Artistic Director, St. Petersburg Opera (1908–17). Bolshoi, Moscow (1916–18). In the 1920s he regularly conducted the London Symphony Orchestra and the orchestra of the Royal Philharmonic

Society. At Covent Garden (1914: 1919–24). Also gave *Ring* with British National Opera Co. and *Boris* with Chaliapin. Organized Coates-Rosing Opera Co. which failed (1936). Also appeared with New York Philharmonic. Conductor Cape Town Municipal Orchestra (1945–53). Too little known in Britain, he did much to introduce Russian music to the West.

COLLINGWOOD, Lawrance, b. 1887, London; d. Montreal, 1952. Also composer. Coates's assistant in St. Petersburg. Joined Old Vic, conducting opera there and Sadler's Wells (1934–35), becoming Principal Conductor at the Wells (1940–46). A heroic figure, succeeding Charles Corri at Sadler's Wells, and working in very difficult circumstances.

COMISSIONA, Sergiu, b. 1928, Bucharest, Romania. Romanian State Ensemble (1948–55). Principal Conductor, Rumanian State Opera (1955–58). Haifa Symphony Orchestra and Israeli Chamber Orchestra (1958–66). Artistic Director, Göteborg Symphony Orchestra (1966–72). Musical Director, Baltimore Symphony Orchestra (1969) and many guest appearances.

CONLON, James, b. New York City, USA. Operatic debut: Spoleto (1971). Metropolitan Opera, New York debut: *Die Zauberflöte* and *La Traviata* (1976). Musical Director, Cincinnati May Festival (1979), and he has conducted many leading American and European orchestras. Covent Garden debut, *Don Carlos* (1979), a considerable personal success. London Symphony Orchestra (1979). A rapidly rising young conductor.

CONSTANT, Marius, b. 1925, Bucharest, Romania. Also a composer. Musical Director, French Radio (1953: 1963–67). Musical Director, Roland Petit Ballet (1956–63). Currently, Director, Ars Nova Ensemble.

CONTA, Iosif, b. 1924, Arad, Romania. Director, Radio Symphony Orchestra (1955–). He has also conducted opera regularly and made many guest appearances abroad.

COOPER, Emil, b. 1877, Kherson, Russia; d. New York, 1960. Kiev Opera (1899–1906). Conducted première of *The Golden Cockerel* in Moscow (1909) and London (1914). Russian seasons in Paris (1909–11). Leaving Russia (1924) he held various posts in Europe, then went to Chicago Opera (1929–32). Metropolitan Opera, New York (1944–50). As well as in Russian music, he excelled in Wagner, conducting the first Russian *Meistersinger* and *Ring*.

CORRI, Charles, b. 1861, London, England; d. London, 1941. One of a family of Anglo-Italian musicians, from 1895–1935 he was Chief Conductor of the Old Vic Opera, then the Sadler's Wells Opera. In circumstances almost unimaginable today, he achieved extraordinary results. There was such a shortage of funds, that when *Tristan* was given, the orchestra could only be *increased* to twenty-eight.

CORTOT, Alfred, b. 1877, Nyon,

Switzerland; d. Lausanne, 1962. The great pianist was also a conductor. He gave the first Parisian *Götterdämmerung* (1902) and much contemporary French music.

COSTA, (Sir) Michael, b. 1808, Naples; d. Hove, England, 1884. Also a composer. Of Spanish descent, he studied in Naples and, later settled in London. Director and Conductor, King's Theatre (1833–46). Became Conductor of Philharmonic Society (1846). Musical Director new Royal Italian Opera, Covent Garden (1847–69). Her Majesty's Opera (1871–79). He also conducted the Birmingham Festival, and the Sacred Harmonic Society. He was a key figure in conducting history, raising standards in Britain immeasurably, notably instilling discipline. Opera was his forte, but all music benefited from him. He would rewrite in the current fashion, his tempos were notably fast, but he forced English musicians to attain the best continental standards. Knighted in 1867.

COWEN, (Sir) Frederick, b. 1852, Kingston, Jamaica; d. London, 1935. Also a composer (who wrote a waltz at six and an operetta at eight) and pianist. Conductor of the Hallé (1888–99). Knighted in 1911.

CZYZ, Henryk, b. 1923, Poland. With Poznan Opera House, then second conductor, Polish Radio Symphony Orchestra (till 1957), going to Lodz Symphony Orchestra. Chief Conductor, Philharmonic Orchestra, Cracow (till 1968), then Generalmusik-direktor, Dusseldorf (1968–71) and Artistic Manager, State Philharmonic Orchestra, Lodz. Has regularly conducted in many European and American cities.

DAMGAARD, Harry, b. 1934, Copenhagen, Denmark. Has conducted all leading Scandinavian orchestras, also Swedish Opera. First Conductor, Finnish National Opera (1975).

DAMROSCH, Leopold, b. 1832, Poznan; d. New York, 1885. Called in to organize a German season at the Metropolitan, New York (1883–84) after its disastrous opening season of Italian opera, he (incredibly) conducted every performance from November 17, 1884 to February 9, 1885, dying a few days later. This feat included the first American *Walküre*. He founded the New York Symphony (1878). His son WALTER DAMROSCH, b. 1862, Breslau, Germany, d. New York, 1950, took over (until 1891). His many premières included the rest of the *Ring* and *Tristan*. He ran his own company (1894), returning to the Metropolitan (1900–03), then concentrating on concerts, education and radio. New York Philharmonic (1902–03). New York Symphony Orchestra (1885–1927), including a tour of Europe.

DANON, Oskar, b. 1913, Sarajevo, now Yugoslavia. Musical Director, Belgrade Opera (1945–63). Has conducted in Chicago, at Edinburgh Festival etc.

DART, Thurston, b. 1921, London, England; d. London, 1971. Also a harpsichordist, organist and musicologist. Artistic Director, Philomusica of London (1955–59).

DAVIES, Meredith, b. 1922, Birkenhead, England. Organist, Choirmaster, Conductor; Three Choirs Festival, Hereford (1949–56). Associate Conductor, City of Birmingham Symphony Orchestra (1957–59)/City of Birmingham Choir (1957–64). Musical Director, English Opera Group (1963–65). Vancouver Symphony Orchestra (1964–71). Conductor, Royal Choral Society (1972–). Has also conducted at Covent Garden.

DAVIES, Noel, b. 1945, London, England. Debut with Kent Opera (1967). English National Opera (1967–78).

DAVIS, Andrew, b. 1944, Ashridge, England. Associate Conductor, BBC Scottish Symphony Orchestra

(1970–72). Associate Conductor, New Philharmonia Orchestra (1973–). Musical Director, Toronto Symphony Orchestra (1975–). A leading Elgarian, he conceived (with Gavin Henderson) the Philharmonia's Elgar Festival (1979), and was its conductor. The event (four orchestral and one chamber concert) was a triumph. Regularly at Glyndebourne Festival (1973–).

DAVIS, Colin, b. 1927, Weybridge, England. The Musical Director of the Royal Opera, Covent Garden (1971–), he is also the Principal Guest Conductor of the Boston Symphony Orchestra and the London Symphony Orchestra. Today's leading conductor of Berlioz, he is also a renowned interpreter of Stravinsky, Mozart, Britten, Tippett and Sibelius, and is becoming a notable Wagnerian. A founder of the Chelsea Opera Group (1950). Assistant Conductor, BBC Scottish Orchestra (1957–59). Sadler's Wells Opera (1960), becoming Musical Director (1961–65). Chief Conductor, BBC Symphony Orchestra (1967–71). After an uneasy start (following Solti), he settled well into his demanding role at Covent Garden, achieving a triumph when the company visited La Scala, Milan (1976). Has also conducted at Glyndebourne and the Metropolitan, New York. In 1979, he led the Royal Opera on a triumphant tour of Japan and Korea. Knighted in 1980.

DAVISON, Arthur, b. Montreal. Also violinist. A wide-ranging career especially in Britain, where he founded the Arthur Davison Concerts for Children at Fairfields Hall, Croydon. Associated with the National Youth Orchestra of Wales and has conducted leading orchestras.

DE ALMEIDA, Antonio, b. 1923, Paris, France. Portuguese Radio (1957–60). Musical Director, Stuttgart Philharmonic (1962–64). Musical Director, Paris Opéra (1964). Guest conductor all over Europe.

DECKER, Franz-Paul, b. 1923, Cologne, Germany. After posts at Cologne, Krefeld and Weisbaden (1945–56), Generalmusikdirektor, Bochum Orchestra (1956–64). Chief Conductor and Artistic Director, Rotterdam Philharmonic (1962–68). Musical Director and Permanent Conductor, Montreal Symphony Orchestra (1967–78).

DE FABRITIIS, Oliviero, b. 1902, Rome, Italy. Rome Opera (1934–61), Conductor and Artistic Secretary (1934–43). Has conducted all over Europe. Conducted first performance of opera in the Roman Baths of Caracalla (1937).

DEFAUW, Désiré, b. 1885, Ghent; d. Gary, Indiana, USA, 1960. Also violinist. Brussels Conservatoire Orchestra (1920–39). Chicago Symphony Orchestra (1943–49).

DE FRANK, Vincent, b. 1915, Long Island, New York, USA. Founder and Conductor, Memphis Symphony Orchestra (1952–). Guest conductor, Memphis Opera Theater, Memphis Ballet Society etc.

DE FROMENT, Louis, b. 1921, Toulouse, France. A leading radio and TV conductor. Permanent Conductor, Radio-Tele-Luxembourg Orchestra (1958–).

DELACOTE, Jacques, b. Nancy, France. His international career began after winning the Mitropoulos Competition in New York (1971), Conducted the New York Philharmonic (1972). London debut with London Symphony Orchestra (Mahler's Third, 1973). *Thaïs* at Wexford (1974). *Faust* at Covent Garden (1976). Conducts American and European orchestras, including the Vienna Symphony, Cleveland and Israel Philharmonic.

DEL MAR, Norman, b. 1919, London, England. Assistant to Beecham, Royal Philharmonic Orchestra (1947). BBC Scottish Orchestra (1960–65) etc., also the biographer of Richard Strauss and a conductor able to handle a Last Night of the Proms.

DE PREIST, James, b. 1936, Philadelphia, Pennsylvania, USA. Debut with New York Philharmonic (1962). Assistant Conductor to Bernstein, New York Philharmonic (1965–66). Associate Conductor, National Symphony Orchestra (1972), Principal Guest Conductor (1975–76). Music Director, Quebec Symphony Orchestra (1976–). Regular guest appearances in North America and Europe.

DE SABATA, Victor, b. 1892, Trieste, Italy; d. S. Margherita, 1967. Also a composer. One of the most thrilling

Victor de Sabata, a supremely exciting conductor of opera and concerts, worshipped by musicians.

operatic conductors of the century, he was second only to Toscanini in his day. Monte Carlo (1919–29), where he conducted the world premières of Ravel's *L'Enfant et les Sortilèges* (1925) and many local premières. La Scala (1929–53), becoming Musical and Artistic Director. *Tristan* at Bayreuth (1939). Led the La Scala company at Covent Garden (1950) in a now legendary season. As well as a great Verdian and Wagnerian, and the conductor of the incomparable Callas–Gobbi–Di Stefano *Tosca* recording of 1953, he was a notable conductor of Beethoven, as Londoners heard in the late '40s. He conducted a very wide range of music in the concert hall as well as the opera house until ill-health forced him to retire in 1953. He emerged to conduct at Toscanini's funeral (1957). For the record, there are those who consider his Bayreuth *Tristan* the greatest they ever heard, while others refuse to place him second to Toscanini.

DESORMIÈRE, Roger, b. 1898, Vichy,

France; d. Paris, 1963. With Diaghilev's Ballet (1925–30). Opéra Comique (1937–46), becoming Musical Director (1944). Ill health forced his early retirement.

DESSOFF, Felix, b. 1835, Leipzig, Germany; d. Frankfurt, 1892. A friend of Brahms, whose First Symphony he conducted at its première (1876). Conductor of the Vienna Philharmonic Orchestra (1861–75).

DE WAART, Edo. See WAART, Edo.

DIETSH, Louis, b. 1808, Dijon, France; d. 1865, Paris. Also composer. Conductor at Paris Opéra (1860–63), but left after a dispute with Verdi. In charge of the *Tannhauser* fiasco (1861).

DILKES, Neville, b. 1930, Derby, England. Founder of English Sinfonia and a regular guest conductor in Britain and abroad. An authority on English music.

DOBROWEN, Issay, b. 1894, Nizhny-Novgorod, Russia; d. Oslo, 1953. Bolshoi, Moscow (1921–22). Dresden (1923). Berlin Volksoper (1924–25). Sofia (1927–28). In USA (1932–35). Budapest Opera (1936–39). Stockholm Royal Opera (1941–45), where he also produced. Conducted Russian operas at La Scala, Milan (1948–53).

DODS, Marcus, b. 1918, Edinburgh, Scotland. Conductor and Chorus Master, Sadler's Wells Opera (1952–58). Principal Conductor BBC Concert Orchestra (1966–69). Musical Director, London Concert Orchestra (1972). Has also conducted opera as a guest conductor, films and musicals.

DOHNANYI, Christoph von, b. 1929, Berlin, Germany. Grandson of the composer, with whom he studied. Musical Director, Lubeck (1957–62), Kassel (1962–64). Generalmusikdirektor, Frankfurt (1968–72). Has also appeared at Salzburg, Berlin, Munich, Metropolitan, New York and Chicago. Premières include Henze's *Der junge Lord* (Berlin, 1965) and *The Bassarids* (Salzburg, 1966). Generalmusikdirektor, Hamburg State Opera (1976–).

DOMINGO, Placido, b. 1941, Madrid, Spain. The great tenor also conducts when his commitments allow – since *Attila* (Barcelona, 1973). Happily for his countless admirers, he is usually too busy singing, but seems destined to enjoy a fine second career.

DORATI, Antal, b. 1906, Budapest, Hungary. Assistant Conductor, Royal Opera House, Budapest (1924–28), then to Dresden. First Conductor, Munster Opera (1928–33) and guest appearances in many other German cities. Musical Director, Ballet Russes de Monte Carlo (with intervals, 1934–41), establishing himself as one of the few major ballet conductors. Musical Director, American Ballet Theater (1941–45), also Director of New Opera Co., New York (1941–42). Organized and directed Dallas Symphony Orchestra (1945–49), Minneapolis Symphony Orchestra (1949–58). Since 1945, guest appearances in USA, Europe, Latin America, Australia and Israel. Chief

Antal Dorati, distinguished not only in the concert hall and in opera, but also in the world of ballet.

Conductor, BBC Symphony Orchestra (1963–67), Chief Conductor, Stockholm Philharmonic Orchestra (1967–74). Musical Director, National Symphony Orchestra (1969). Royal Philharmonic Orchestra (1974–), also Musical Director of Detroit Symphony Orchestra (1976–). Conductor Laureate, Royal Philharmonic Orchestra (1980–). His *Notes of Seven Decades* (1980) has been widely praised and enjoyed.

DOWNES, Edward, b. 1926, Birmingham, England. Originally a horn player. A very experienced opera conductor. Joined Covent Garden (1952) until becoming the first Musical Director of Australian Opera (1972–76). Though noted for his wide repertoire and his Wagner and Verdi, he is particularly well-known for his Russian performances, including the first British *Katerina Ismailova* (Covent Garden) and *War and Peace*, with which the Australian Opera opened at the Sydney Opera House.

DREIER, Per, b. 1929, Tronheim, Norway. Chief Conductor, Jutland Symphony Orchestra (1957–71). Chief Conductor and Artistic Director, Aarhus Symphony Orchestra (1957–73) and many guest appearances abroad.

DUTOIT, Charles, b. 1936, Switzerland. Musical Director and Principal Conductor, Montreal Symphony Orchestra (1979–) having previously been Musical Director of the Berne Symphony, Göteborg. Symphony and National Symphony Orchestra of Mexico. Earlier he worked with Karajan and Kempe. A regular guest conductor in many countries. During 1980–81, he will conduct concerts at La Scala, Milan, and with the Berlin Philharmonic.

E

EHRLING, Sixten, b. 1918, Malmö, Sweden. Stockholm, Royal Opera (1940–60), Chief Conductor and Musical Director from 1953. Musical Director and Conductor, Detroit Symphony Orchestra (1963–73). Has conducted opera and concerts in New York, including at the Metropolitan Opera.

EICHINGER, Hans, b. 1902, Vienna, Austria. After posts in Germany, was with Stockholm Philharmonic and Swedish Radio Orchestras (1946–65), also with Norrköping Symphony Orchestra (1949–54). Guest Conductor, Radio Vienna (1958–64). Has also conducted in Athens etc.

ELDER, Mark, b. 1947, Hexham, England. After working at Glyndebourne and Covent Garden, he went to Sydney, Australia (1972) for two years with Australian Opera. With English National Opera (1975–), conducting a very wide range of works, then, suddenly, becoming Musical Director (1979) owing to the retirement of Sir Charles Groves. He has also conducted leading British symphony orchestras. Conducting debut at the Royal Opera House, Covent Garden, with *Rigoletto* (1976).

His elevation at the ENO has been widely acclaimed. To conduct *Meistersinger* at Bayreuth (1981).

EPSTEIN, David, b. 1930, New York City, USA. Also a composer. Many guest engagements in Europe and North America. Musical Director and Conductor of Harrisburg Symphony Orchestra.

ERDELYI, Miktos, b. 1928, Budapest, Hungary. Leading Hungarian conductor, notably of opera.

EREDE, Alberto, b. 1909, Genoa, Italy. After working with Weingartner and Busch, he made his operatic debut with the *Ring* in Turin (1935). At Glyndebourne before the war, becoming Musical Director of the New London Opera Company (1946–48). At the Metropolitan, New York (1950–54). Deutsche Oper am Rhein (1956–62), becoming Generalmusikdirektor (1958). *Lohengrin* at Bayreuth (1962). He has conducted in many leading opera houses. His seasons in London with the New London company at the Cambridge Theatre, unforgotten by older operagoers, proved his brilliance as a trainer of singers and creator of a true ensemble almost from scratch.

ERICSON, Eric, b. 1918, Sweden. Leading choral conductor at home (especially on radio) and abroad. Conducted Bergman's notable film of *The Magic Flute*.

ERMERT, Herbert, b. 1936, Siegerland, Germany. Conductor of Bonn Bach Choir and Siegerland Oratorio Choir, touring abroad with them. Has also conducted leading German, French and Belgian orchestras. London debut with Royal Philharmonic Orchestra (1979).

EROS, Peter, b. 1932, Budapest, Hungary. Associate Conductor, Concertgebouw, Amsterdam (1960–65). Chief Conductor, Malmo Symphony Orchestra (1967–69). Musical Director, San Diego Symphony Orchestra (1972). A guest conductor in USA, Britain, Europe, Australia, South America and Israel.

ESSER, Heinrich, b. 1818, Mannheim, Germany; d. Salzburg, Austria, 1872. Also composer. Musical Director, Court Theatre Mannheim (1838). At Mainz, then Kappellmeister at the Imperial Opera, Vienna (1847–69). Though not a committed Wagnerian, he was an able and consciencious interpreter of his music.

FACCIO, Franco, b. 1840, Verona, Italy; d. Monza, Italy, 1891. Also a composer. One of the leading Italian conductors of his day (from the 1870s, before which he was best known as a composer). At La Scala, Milan (1871–90), where his premières included *Otello, La Gioconda* and Puccini's *Edgar*, also Milan's first Wagnerian opera, *Lohengrin* (1873). Conducted London's first *Otello* (1889).

FAILONI, Sergeo, b. 1890, Verona, Italy; d. Sopron, Hungary, 1948. Many posts in Italy, including La Scala (1932–34: 1940–41: 1946–47) and the Verona Arena. Musical Director, Budapest State Opera (1928–47).

FARIS, Alexander, b. 1921, Caledon, Northern Ireland. Also a composer. Royal Ballet (1960–61). Sadler's Wells Opera (1960–69). Has conducted and orchestrated a number of West End Musicals.

FARNCOMBE, Charles, b. 1919, London, England. Musical Director, Handel Opera Society (1955–), and has played a leading part in restoring Handel's operas to the stage. Musical Director, Drottningholm Court Theatre, Stockholm (1969–).

FASANO, Renato, b. 1902, Naples, Italy; d. Rome, 1979. Founder of the Collegium Musicum Italicum in Rome (1941) and the Virtuosi di Roma, also the Piccolo Teatro Musicale Italiano (1957). With his disciplined organizations, he has toured widely at home, all over Europe and in the USA. His services to 17th, 18th and early 19th century music, orchestral and operatic, have been incomparable.

FELDBRILL, Victor, b. 1924, Toronto, Canada. Music Director, Winnipeg Symphony Orchestra (1958–68). Has conducted all major Canadian orchestras, also many European orchestras, including the BBC Symphony Orchestra. Appointed Resident Conductor, Toronto Symphony Orchestra (1973).

FERENCSIK, János, b. 1907, Hungary. Budapest Opera (1927–). Musical Director since 1950. Musical Director, Hungarian State Philharmonic Orchestra. Many guest appearances abroad in Europe and USA, including San Francisco Opera (1962–63) and Edinburgh Festival (1963: 1973). The doyen of Hungarian conductors.

FIEDLER, Arthur, b. Boston, 1894; d.

1979. Originally a violinist with the Boston Symphony Orchestra, he was (from 1930), the conductor of the Boston Pops Orchestra, becoming, like his concerts, an American Institution.

FISTOULARI, Anatole, b. 1907, Kiev, Russia. After conducting in Russia – he was a seven-year-old prodigy – he came West (1920), conducting regularly in Western Europe. Grand Opera Rousse (Paris, 1931), then with Ballet de Monte Carlo on its many tours. Principal Conductor, London Philharmonic Orchestra (1943–44). Founder of London International Orchestra (1946). Has conducted widely in Europe, the Americas, Africa and Israel.

FJELDSTAD, Øivin, b. 1903, Norway. Began as a violinist. Chief Conductor Norwegian State Broadcasting (1945–62). Norwegian State Opera Orchestra (1958–59). Musical Director and Chief Conductor, Oslo Philharmonic Orchestra (1962–74). Has conducted widely abroad.

FOGELL, Martin, b. 1929, Glasgow, Scotland. Also composer. Has been conductor of many regional groups, also Conductor, Fogell Ensemble (1954–60) and Music Director and Principal Conductor, London Students Opera Co. (1966–71). Guest conductor in Britain and Europe.

FOSS, Lukas, b. 1922, Berlin, Germany. Also composer and pianist. Posts include Buffalo Philharmonic (1963–70). Has conducted Berlin Philharmonic, Israel Philharmonic, Leningrad Philharmonic etc., and is a leading exponent of avant garde music.

FOSTER, Lawrence, b. 1941, Los Angeles, California, USA. Associate Conductor, San Francisco Ballet (1960–65). Assistant Conductor, Los Angeles Philharmonic Orchestra (1965–68). Guest Conductor, Royal Philharmonic Orchestra (1969–74). Music Director, Houston Philharmonic Orchestra (1971–). Has conducted widely in USA and abroad. Debut at Covent Garden, *Troilus and Cressida* (1976), and has also conducted Scottish Opera and opera in Houston, Washington and Los Angeles. A notable exponent of modern American and English music. Resident Conductor, Monte Carlo Opera Orchestra (1980–).

FRANCIS, Alun, b. 1943, Kidderminster. Also a composer. Made his name in the 1970s as Artistic Director and Conductor of the Ulster Orchestra and the Northern Ireland Opera Trust, as a noted interpreter of Donizetti, and a wide-ranging guest conductor of British, European, American and other orchestras.

FRANKLE, Hubert, b. 1930, Geneva, Switzerland. Also composer. Posts have included Suisse Romande Orchestra (Radio Geneva), for Geneva City (1958–63) and many leading choirs.

FRECCIA, Massimo, b. Florence, Italy. Musical Director and Chief Conductor, Havana Symphony Orchestra (1939–43) and New Orleans Symphony Orchestra (1944–52), also

Baltimore Symphony Orchestra (1952–59). Chief Conductor, RAI Radiotelevisione Orchestra, Rome (1959–65). Guest appearances in many countries, including seven seasons with New York Philharmonic at Toscanini's invitation.

FREDMAN, Myer, b. 1932, Dalrymple, Queensland, Australia. Glyndebourne music staff (1959–73), becoming First Conductor and Head of Music Staff, also Musical Director, Glyndeboune Touring Opera. Musical Director, State Opera of South Australia (1973–80), giving the Australian premières of Tippett's *A Midsummer Marriage* and Britten's *Death in Venice*. He has conducted opera in Brussels, Germany, Rumania and the Wexford Festival, including Mozart, Verdi and Strauss, and many orchestras in Britain and abroad, playing much British music.

FRÉMAUX, Louis, b. 1921, Air-sur-Lys, France. Chief Conductor, National Opera of Monte Carlo (1956–66). Director, Rhône-Alpes Philharmonic Orchestra (1969–). Chief Conductor, City of Birmingham Symphony Orchestra (1969–78).

FRICSAY, Ferenc, b. 1914, Budapest, Hungary; d. Basle, Switzerland, 1963. First Conductor, Budapest Opera (1939–45). Conducted première of Einem's *Dantons Tod* (Salzburg, 1947). Director, Berlin Städtische Oper (1951–52), resigning after dispute with management. Munich State Opera (1956–58), returning to Berlin to new Deutsches Opernhaus (1961). A very fine conductor, pupil of Bartok and Kodaly.

FRIEND, Lionel, b. 1945, London, England. Welsh National Opera (1968–72). Glyndebourne (1969–72). Second Kapellmeister, Staatstheater (1972–75). English National Opera (1977–). Has conducted Proms (1977–) and at festivals, including Bath and Cheltenham. Regularly conducts BBC orchestras and others. A noted conductor of modern music.

FRUHBECK de BURGOS, Rafael, b. 1933, Burgos, Spain. Chief Conductor, Municipal Orchestra, Bilbao (1958–62). Musical Director and Chief Conductor, Spanish National Orchestra, Madrid (1962–77). Musical Director and Chief Conductor, Dusseldorf Symphoniker (1966).

FUCHS, Peter Paul, b. 1916, Vienna, Austria. To USA (1941), on staff of Metropolitan, New York for ten years, also with other opera companies. Musical Director, Baton Rouge Symphony Orchestra (1962–) and other US posts, and has also conducted in Europe.

FURST, Janos, b. Budapest. Began as violinist, founding Irish Chamber Orchestra (1963). Has conducted most leading British orchestras in '70s. Chief Conductor, Malmö Symphony Orchestra (1974–77), then becoming its Chief Guest Conductor. Has also conducted opera in Malmö. Tokyo Philharmonic Orchestra (1976–) as guest conductor. Danish Radio (1978–). Also conducts regularly in France, Holland and Mexico.

FURTWÄNGLER, Wilhelm, b. 1886, Berlin, Germany; d. Baden-Baden, Germany, 1954. There are many who fervently believe that this constroversial conductor was the greatest of his day, despite a notorious beat, nightmarishly hard to follow. When he made his debut in Florence, one of the orchestra was so amazed by his convolutions that he called out: 'Coraggio, Maestro!' Words used about him include mystic, visionary, idealist, and, certainly, conducting technique was no concern of his. He could appear to be hypnotized while conducting. So great was the intensity he brought to the podium that he cast a spell, which few of his recordings capture. Though the spell was no help to musicians trying to follow his beat, most of them loved playing under him, especially the great German 19th century masterpieces. He could never explain himself verbally, yet, as thousands can recall, miracles occurred when he conducted.

After engagements at Zurich, Strasbourg and Lubeck, Furtwängler made his name at Mannheim (1915–20), then in Berlin and Vienna. He succeeded Nikisch with the Berlin Philharmonic (1922–54) and at the Leipzig Gewandhaus (1922–29). Though mainly in the concert hall at this time, he conducted at Bayreuth (1931: 1936–1937: 1943–44), *Tristan* at Covent Garden (1935) also the *Ring* (1937–38). He regularly conducted at Salzburg and in Vienna, also Wagner at La Scala. His role in Nazi Germany remains notorious. Never anti-Jewish as such, he kept Jews in employment and played Hindemith's *Mathis der Maler*, though the composer was violently abused for it and later the work was banned. Furtwängler gave up his Berlin posts, was offered the job of succeeding Toscanini with the New York Philharmonic (1936), but had to turn it down because of American Jewish opinion. He stayed in Germany believing he could keep out of politics, but he was an unhappy man. After the war, Britain allowed him to return, but he was kept out of the USA: he had made his debut with the New York Philharmonic in 1925. He returned to London with the Vienna Philharmonic, then conducted the London Philharmonic Orchestra and the Philharmonia. He collapsed during a Vienna concert (1953). He was also a composer, ambitious but sadly unsuccessful.

Wilhelm Furtwängler's reputation continues to soar a quarter of a century after his death.

GABRILOWITSCH, Ossip, b. 1878, St. Petersburg, Russia; d. Detroit, USA 1936. Also a very famous pianist. Conductor, Detroit Orchestra (1917–35), also appearing with the Philadelphia Orchestra.

GALLIERA, Alceo, b. 1910, Milan, Italy. Also a composer. Resident Conductor, Teatro Carlo Felice, Genoa (1957–60), later becoming Resident conductor, Orchestre Municipale de Strasbourg. Guest appearances in many countries.

GAMBA, Pierino, b. 1937, Rome, Italy. A child prodigy conductor, he made his debut at eight and toured widely. Surviving the transition to adulthood, his wide-ranging career has included very successful visits to Britain, France and the USA, and a long engagement as Conductor of the Winnipeg Symphony Orchestra for much of the 1970s.

GAMSON, Arnold, b. 1926, Greenwich, Conn., USA. Musical Director, American Opera Society (1951–62). Assistant Conductor, New York Philharmonic (1961). Artistic Director, Amici del Opera of Rome.

Guest appearances in USA, Mexico and Italy.

GARDELLI, Lamberto, b. 1915, Venice, Italy. Began as double-bass player. Also a composer. Best known as a champion of early Verdi, having recorded many of the operas. Guest conductor, Royal Swedish Opera, Stockholm (1946–55), when he became permanent conductor of Danish Radio. Budapest Opera (1961–65). Glyndebourne (1964–65: 1968). Metropolitan, New York (1966–68) and regularly at Covent Garden (1968–). Also Deutsche Oper, Berlin and concerts in many European and American cities.

GARDINER, John Eliot, b. 1928, Oxford, England. Also organist, choirmaster and writer. A notable expert on 17th and 18th century music, especially French opera, he has conducted most leading British and many European orchestras. Musical Director of Monteverdi Choir and Orchestra. Artistic Director, Göttingen Handel Festival (1981–83).

GAUBERT, Phillipe, b. 1879, Cahors, France; d. Paris, 1941. Also composer.

Principal Conductor, Paris Opéra (1920–41).

GAVAZZENI, Gianandrea, b. 1919, Bergamo, Italy. Also a composer. La Scala, Milan (1948–). Artistic Director (1966–68), and has appeared with the company in Edinburgh, Montreal, Russia and Brussels. Also a critic and biographer.

GELLHORN, Peter, b. 1912, Breslau, Germany. Also pianist and composer. Sadler's Wells and Carl Rosa Operas (1941–46). Conductor and Head of Music Staff, Covent Garden (1947–53). Glyndebourne (1954–61: 1974–). Director, BBC Chorus (1961–72). Co-Founder and Musical Director, Opera Barga, Italy (1967–69).

GERICKE, Wilhelm, b. 1845, Graz, Austria; d. Vienna, 1925. After posts in Linz and Vienna, became Conductor of Boston Symphony Orchestra (1884–89: 1898–1906). Summed up by Harold Schonberg as a 'cold, precise disciplinarian.'

GHYOROS, Julien, b. 1922, Liège, Belgium. Liège Orchestra (1960–63). First ConductorOpera of Liège (1963–65). Has conducted widely in Belgium, Germany, France etc.

GIBSON, (Sir) Alexander, b. 1926, Motherwell, Scotland. Sadler's Wells Opera (1951–59), becoming Musical Director (1957–59). Assistant Conductor, BBC Scottish Orchestra (1952–54). Principal Conductor and Musical Director, Scottish National Orchestra (1959–). Artistic Director, Scottish Opera (1962–). He founded Scottish Opera, determined that it should reach high standards from the start (which it did). It is one of the greatest success stories in British operatic history. A wide-ranging conductor, excellent with singers, his achievements can best be seen in the renown which Scottish Opera enjoys. He has over sixty operas in his repertoire. Knighted in 1977.

GIELEN, Michael, b. 1927, Dresden, Germany. Colon Theatre, Buenos Aires (1947–50). Vienna Staatsoper (1950–60). Music Director, Royal Opera, Stockholm (1960–65). Netherlands Opera (1972–77). Principal Guest Conductor, BBC Symphony Orchestra (1978–). Musical Director, Frankfurt Opera (1977–). He has conducted widely including concerts with the New York Philharmonic (1973–). Musical Director, Cincinnati Symphony Orchestra (1980–).

GIERSTER, Hans, b. 1925, Germany. Generalmusikdirektor, Municipal theatres, Nuremberg (1956–) and has regularly guest conducted at home and abroad. Musical Director, Nuremberg Opera (1965–).

GIMÉNEZ, Jeronimo, b. 1854, Seville, Spain; d. Madrid, 1923. Also composer. Director of Apollo Theatre, Madrid (1885), then Madrid's Zarazuela Theatre, where he conducted many zarazuelas and the first Spanish *Carmen*.

GIOVANINETTI, Reynald, b. 1932, Sétif, Algeria. Leading French conductor. Artistic Director Marseilles

Opera (1972), later conducting opera in Canada, Italy and elsewhere, also concerts.

GIULINI, Carlo Maria, b. 1914, Barletta, Italy. Originally a viola player. This renowned conductor's first post was Musical Director, Radio Italiana (1946–51), after which he joined La Scala, Milan (1951–56). He rapidly made his name as one of the finest young conductors of the day, notably in Callas performances. Regularly at Covent Garden (1958–67) where his (and Visconti's) legendary *Don Carlos* was not only one of the theatre's greatest triumphs, but also established the work as a popular favourite and proved Giulini to be an outstanding Verdian. He also conducted at leading festivals – Edinburgh, Aix, Florence and Holland – and gave memorable concerts with the Philharmonia. Tragically (for opera), he became dissatisfied with operatic conditions, particularly some of the producers, from the mid-1960s, and returned to opera less and less, though sometimes working with Visconti. Musical Director of the Los Angeles Philharmonic Orchestra (1978–), with which he at once made a great impact. A return to opera on his conditions is reported at the time of writing. An inspirational, deeply serious musician, totally at the service of the composer.

GODFREY, (Sir) Dan, b. 1868, London, England; d. Bournemouth 1939. Born into a family of military bandmasters, he is best remembered for his work as Conductor of the Bournemouth Municipal Orchestra (1893–1934), where he introduced many British compositions. Knighted in 1922.

GODFREY, Isidore, b. 1900, London, England; d. 1977. Musical Director, D'Oyly Carte Opera (1929–68).

GOEHR, Walter, b. 1903, Berlin, Germany; d. Sheffield, England, 1960. Also composer. Held various posts in Germany. With German Radio (1925–31), writing the first radio opera, *Malpopita*. BBC Theatre Orchestra (1946–49), and a regular guest conductor. He helped revive interest in Purcell and Monteverdi. His son is the composer Alexander Goehr.

GOERTZ, Harald, b. 1924, Vienna, Austria. Also pianist. Conductor, Vienna Boys Choir (1947–48). State Opera, Ankara, Turkey (1948–50). Musical Director, opera and concerts, Ulm (1955–63) and many guest appearances including with Stuttgart Opera and the Berlin Philharmonic.

GOLDSCHMIDT, Berthold, b. 1903, Hamburg, Germany. Also composer. Assistant Conductor, Berlin Staatsoper (1926–27). Conductor, Darmstadt Opera (1927–29). Artistic Adviser, Berlin Städtische Oper (1931–33).

GOMEZ-MARTINEZ, Miguel, b. 1949, Granada, Spain. Deutsche Oper, Berlin (1974–76). Vienna State Opera (1977–), with guest appearances at Covent Garden and many European centres.

GOODALL, Reginald, b. 1905, Lincoln, England. This famous

Wagnerian was assistant to Coates at Covent Garden (1936–39), later assistant to Sargent with the Royal Choral Society. Sadler's Wells Opera (1944–45), conducting the première of *Peter Grimes*. Joined the new Covent Garden Opera (1946–). For many years conducted Italian opera, which was not his school, plus the occasional *Boris*, Britten, and fine performances of *Wozzeck*, also the very occasional Wagner, mainly on tour, except for some *Meistersinger* performances in the '50s. Otherwise he coached. The breakthrough came with the Sadler's Wells *Mastersingers* (1968) since when his *Ring* and other performances with the company, now the English National Opera, have revealed a great Wagnerian. Peter Heyworth has written of the 'indefinable blend of majesty and lyrical radiance' of his interpretations, though a minority has found his tempos too slow. He has been able to inspire the company's orchestra and casts to great heights. Another triumph: *Tristan und Isolde* with the Welsh National Opera (1979).

GOOSSENS, Eugène I, b. 1845, Bruges, Belgium; d. Liverpool, England, 1906. He became a leading English conductor (from 1873). With Carl Rosa (from 1882). Eugène II, b. 1867, Bordeaux, France; d. London, 1958. Worked with his father with Carl Rosa, then for other touring opera cos. Principal Conductor, Carl Rosa (1899–1915). With Beecham Co. (1917–18). Eugène III, b. 1893, London, England; d. London, 1962. Also composer. With Carl Rosa, Beecham Co., British National Opera Co. etc. also conducted ballet. Assistant Conductor, Rochester Philharmonic (1923). Principal Conductor, Cincinnati Orchestra (1931–46), and guest appearances with Philadelphia Orchestra, New York Philharmonic, Berlin Philharmonic and Royal Philharmonic Society concerts. In Australia (1947–56) as Conductor of Sydney Symphony Orchestra. Director of New South Wales Conservatory of Music (1947–56). Conducted his operas *Judith* (Covent Garden, 1929) and *Don Juan de Manara* (Covent Garden, 1937 and in Philadelphia, 1930s).

GRAY, Harold, b. Birmingham, 1908. Assistant Conductor, City of Birmingham Symphony Orchestra (1929–39). Music Adviser, Western Command during Second World War, forming Symphony Orchestra of enlisted professionals. Principal Conductor, Carl Rosa Opera (1944–46). Associate Conductor, City of Birmingham Symphony Orchestra (1947–79), conducting final Prom, an emotional occasion for audience and conductor alike. Now Conductor Emeritus for life.

GREGOR, Bohumil, b. 1911, Praha, Czechoslovakia. Posts have included Chief Conductor, National Theatre, Prague. Has conducted widely abroad and recorded the complete works of Janáček.

GROVES, (Sir) Charles, b. 1915, London, England. BBC Northern Symphony Orchestra (1944–51). Bournemouth Symphony Orchestra (1951–61). Welsh National Opera (1961–63). Later with the Royal Liverpool Philharmonic Orchestra and Associate Conductor, Royal Philharmonic Orchestra. Musical Director, English National Opera (1978–79), having been a guest conductor with the co. since 1971. His premières include Crosse's *Story of Vasco* (1974) and the first British *Euryanthe* (1977). A sound conductor whose operatic reputation is rising, though for health reasons he had to retire from his ENO post (1979), becoming instead a guest conductor once again. Knighted in 1973.

GRUNEBAUM, Hermann, b. 1872, Giessen, Germany; d. Chipstead, England, 1954. After posts in Germany, Chorus Master, Covent Garden (1907–33). Co-founder of London School of Opera, conducted première of Holst's *Savitri* (1916). Director of opera class, Royal College of Music: gave complete *Parsifal* with students, co-conducting with Boult (1926).

GUADAGNO, Anton, b. 1925, Castellammare de Golfo, Italy. Also composer. Currently, leading Italian conductor at Vienna State Opera. He has also conducted in Italy, Germany, USA and at Covent Garden.

GUARNIERI, Antonio, b. 1880, Venice, Italy; d. Milan, 1952. La Scala, Milan (1922–23: 1929–52). Regarded as a very fine musician.

GUHR, Carl Wilhelm, b. 1787, Militisch, Germany; d. Frankfurt, 1848. A showman conductor at Frankfurt in the 1840s, he added

military bands to his orchestra for Haydn's *Creation* for 'Let there be light', and not content with a shattering chord, he had the gas jets turned up in the hall on the word 'light'. Remembered for little else!

GUI, Vittorio, b. 1885, Rome, Italy; d. Florence, 1975. One of the outstanding Italian conductors of the century, he founded the Florence Orchestra (1928), which led to the creation of the Maggio Musicale (1933–). La Scala, Milan (1923–25: 1932–34). Founder of the Teatro di Torino (1925). Covent Garden (1938–39: 1952) and, most notably in Britain, was at Glyndebourne (1952–65) as Chief Conductor and, later, as Head of Music and Artistic Counsellor. A renowned conductor of Gluck, Mozart and Rossini, indeed Gui was chiefly responsible for the Rossini revival in the 1920s and 1930s in Italy and later elsewhere. He was also a superb conductor of Bellini and Verdi, also of *Pelléas et Mélisande* (Glyndebourne, 1962). In Florence he revived interest in Spontini and Cherubini, also giving a famous *Khovanschina* (1948), while in 1972, so affronted was he by the cast and production of a Rome *Traviata* that he walked out.

GUIDI-DREI, Claudio, b. 1927, Buenos Aires, Argentina. Also a composer. With Argentina Theatre, La Plata (1960–73), finally as Artistic Director/Orchestral Director, Colon Theatre, Buenos Aires, also a regular radio conductor.

H

HABENECK, Francois, b. 1781, Mezières, France; d. Paris, 1849. Also a composer and violinist. He founded the Société des Concerts du Conservatoire (1828). This last of the violin conductors and first modern French conductor, was admired by Wagner. He introduced Beethoven's symphonies to France, and Wagner noted that the Ninth was played as written and how good Habeneck's players were. Alas, the conductor is best remembered because of his less than fortunate brushes with Berlioz, as described by the composer in his *Memoirs*. See Chapter 1.

HADLEY, Henry, b. 1871, Somerville, Mass., USA; d. New York, 1937. Also a composer. The founder of the Berkshire Music Festival (1933). Conducted in Seattle, San Francisco and New York and composed operas and symphonies.

HAITINK, Bernard, b. 1929, Amsterdam, Holland. Netherlands Radio Philharmonic Orchestra (1955–61). Guest Conductor, Concertgebouw Orchestra, Amsterdam (1956–6), later becoming Joint Conductor, then Musical Director. Principal Conductor and Adviser, London Philharmonic Orchestra (1967–70), Artistic Adviser (1970–80). Regular guest conductor with Hallé, Los Angeles Philharmonic, Berlin Philharmonic. Musical Director of Glyndebourne Festival Opera (1978–). One of the finest and most musicianly conductors of the post-war era, he is famous for his mastery of the 19th century symphonic repertoire. Until his Glyndebourne debut (*The Rake's Progress*, 1976), he had conducted little opera, but has rapidly established himself as a leading operatic conductor, and proved a superb Mozartian.

HALÁSZ, László, b. 1905, Debrecen, Hungary. Originally a pianist, he became a conductor and manager. Posts include Budapest (1929–30), Prague (1930–32), Vienna (1933–36) and Salzburg (1929–36). *Tristan* at St. Louis (1936). Director, St. Louis Grand Opera Association (1939–42). New York City Center Opera (1943–51). After difficulties with the management, was dismissed and returned to Europe to conduct.

HALLÉ, (Sir) Charles, b. 1819, Hagen, Germany; d. Manchester, 1895. Also a pianist. His greatest achievement was the founding of the Hallé Orchestra in Manchester (1857), which he conducted until his death. Settled in Manchester (1848), conducting opera there (1854–55) and in London at Her Majesty's (1860–61). As well as his work with the Hallé, he founded the Royal Manchester College of Music (1893). Knighted in 1888.

HALLMAN, Ludlow, b. 1941, Dayton, Ohio, USA. Has conducted widely in the US, including Santa Fé Opera, also in Salzburg. Posts have included Musical Director and Conductor, Salzburg Baroque Ensemble.

HALSEY, Louis, b. 1929, London, England. Founder and Conductor, the Elizabethan Singers (1953–66) and Louis Halsey Singers (1967–), also Thames Chamber Choir.

HANDFORD, Maurice, b. 1929, Salisbury, England. Associate Conductor Hallé Orchestra (1960–71). Staff Conductor, City of Birmingham Symphony Orchestra. A guest conductor in Europe and the Americas.

HANDLEY, Vernon, b. 1930, Enfield, England. Debut with Bournemouth Symphony Orchestra (1961), since when he has been a guest conductor

Bernard Haitink, master of the 19th century symphonic repertoire and now a major opera conductor.

with nearly all the leading British orchestras.

HARTY, (Sir) Hamilton, b. 1879, Hillsborough, Ireland; d. Hove, England, 1941. Best known today for his arrangements of Handel's *Water Music* and *Music for the Royal Fireworks*, his most famous conducting post was with the Hallé (1920–33), which he rapidly rebuilt after the war years. The foremost conductor of Berlioz of his day. Knighted in 1925.

HASSELMANS, Louis, b. 1878, Paris, France; d. San Juan, 1957. Best known as an opera conductor, notably at Montreal (1911–13), Chicago (1918–20) and the Metropolitan, New York (1921–36).

HAUSEGGER, Siegmund von, b. 1872, Graz, Austria; d. Munich, 1948. Also a composer. Posts included Munich National Theatre (1922–23) and Director of Munich Academy of Music (1922–26).

HEALD-SMITH, Geoffrey, b. 1930, Mexborough, England. A leading figure in North-East England music, notably Conductor of Hull City Youth Orchestra and as Chief Conductor, Yorkshire Concert Orchestra. Has conducted in Austria, Switzerland, Germany and Norway.

HEGER, Robert, b. 1886, Strasbourg, (then in) Germany; d. Munich 1978. Also composer. His many posts included Vienna State Opera (1925–33), Berlin Staatsoper (1933–34), Berlin Städtische Oper (1944–50). At Covent Garden (1925–35) and with Munich

company (1953), giving the first London *Capriccio* (Richard Strauss).

HEINRICH, Siegfried, b. 1935, Dresden, Germany. Artistic Director, Hersfeld Festival Concerts (1961–) and has conducted widely in Europe, also in Japan.

HEINZE (Sir) Bernard, b. 1894, Shepperton, Australia. The leading Australian conductor, he was Director-General of Music, Australian Broadcasting Commission (1929–32) and has been Conductor, Royal Melbourne Philharmonic Society (1928–), also Conductor, Melbourne Symphony Orchestra (1933–46). Other posts include Director, State Conservatory of New South Wales (1957–66) and Conductor, Victorian Symphony Orchestra.

HERBIG, Gunther, b. 1931, Usti nad Labem, Czechoslovakia. General-musikdirektor and Principal Conductor, Dresden Philharmonic Orchestra (1972–77), Principal Guest Conductor, BBC Northern Symphony Orchestra (1979–). Principal Guest Conductor, Dallas Symphony Orchestra (1979–) after successful American debut there (1977–78).

HERTZ, Alfred, b. 1872, Frankfurt, Germany; d. San Francisco, USA, 1947. After conducting in Germany, he was at the Metropolitan, New York (1902–15) in charge of German opera. Gave the first American *Parsifal* without Cosima Wagner's permission (1903), so was barred from all German opera houses. San Francisco Orchestra (1915–30), also conducting the Opera there and in Los Angeles. A big, belligerent man, he was a cripple from polio. Gave the American premières of *Rosenkavalier* and *Salome*, and, not surprisingly, became a US citizen.

HEWARD, Leslie, b. 1897, Liversedge, England; d. Birmingham, 1943. A distinguished conductor who died young. City of Birmingham Symphony Orchestra (1930–43).

HICKOX, Richard, b. 1948, Stokenchurch. Musical Director, Richard Hickox Singers and Orchestra, now the City of London Sinfonia. Director of London Symphony Chorus.

HILLER, Ferdinand von, b. 1811, Frankfurt; d. Cologne, 1885. Also pianist and composer. A careless and indifferent conductor, according to Wagner, he was devoted to slow tempos. Conducted the Leipzig Gewandhaus (1843–44). More valuable were his writings on his contemporaries.

HIMMEL, Friedrich, b. 1765, Brandenburg, Germany; d. Berlin, 1814. Best known – in his day – as a composer. Conductor of the Berlin Opera (1800–14).

HOESSLIN, Franz von, b. 1885, Munich, Germany; d. nr. Sète, France (in an air crash), 1946. Well-known in Germany as an opera conductor: Mannheim, Berlin, Breslau etc. Bayreuth (1927–28: 1934: 1938–40).

HOFFMAN, Irwin, b. 1924, New York City, USA. Vancouver Symphony Orchestra, British Columbia (1952–64). Associate Conductor and Acting Musical Director, Chicago Symphony Orchestra (1964–70). Florida Gulf Coast Symphony Orchestra (1968). Chief Permanent Conductor, Belgian Radio and TV Symphony Orchestra (1972). Wide-ranging guest conductor.

HOFMAN, Hermann, b. 1922, Karlsruhe, Germany. Also composer. Musical Director, Palatinate Chamber Orchestra, Mannheim-Ludwigshafen (1959–).

HOGWOOD, Christopher, b. 1941, Nottingham, England. This distingushed harpsichordist, lecturer and musicologist, and founder of the Academy of Ancient Music (1973), is also a regular conductor. Conducted his first Prom in 1978, the year he began his ambitious project to record the complete Mozart symphonies in authentic versions on late 18th century instruments.

HOLST, Imogen, b. 1907, Richmond, Surrey, England. The daughter of Gustave Holst, she has performed his music regularly in concerts and on records. Also a lecturer and writer on music.

HORENSTEIN, Jasha, b. 1898, Kiev, Russia; d. London, 1973. After posts in Vienna and Berlin, he became Musical Director, Dusseldorf Opera (1929–33), leaving because of the Nazis. Became a guest conductor in France, Scandinavia etc. settling in USA (1941). He conducted widely there and in South America, later in Europe, where he settled in Switzerland. Renowned for his Bruckner and Mahler. His final performance was *Parsifal* at Covent Garden just before he died.

HOWARTH, Elgar, b. 1935, Lancashire, England. Originally a trumpeter, he has been conducting since 1969, with all leading British Orchestras, also in Scandinavia, Germany etc. Regularly at the Proms. He has turned more and more to opera, including a notable *Nabucco* (1980) for English National North, also in Stockholm, Hamburg etc. To conduct *Boris Godonov* for Australian Opera (1980) and at Glyndebourne (1981). Also a composer and an expert on brass band music, having done much serious pioneer work in the genre.

HUBAD, Samo, b. 1917, Ljublijana, Yugoslavia. Opera House, Ljublijana (1941–56), since when leading posts have included Zagreb Opera (1958–64) and Conductor, Slovenian Philharmonic Orchestra (1980–   ).

HUDEZ, Karl, b. 1904, Salzburg, Austria. Max Reinhardt Productions (1924–38). Salzburg Festival (1928–60). Music Director, Vienna People's Opera (1938–44). Director of Studies, Vienna State Opera (1953–68). Has also run courses in Finland.

HUDSON, Derek, b. 1934, Hove, England. Musical Director, Chichester Festival Theatre (1963–64: 1966). Musical Director, Centre 42 and London Dance Centre (1964). Royal Ballet (1965). Guest conductor with leading British orchestras. Musical Director, Cape Town Symphony Orchestra (1967–72). Director, Bulawayo Philharmonic Orchestra, Rhodesia (1974).

HURST, George, b. 1926, Rumanian father and Russian mother. York Symphony Orchestra, Pennsylvania (1950–55). Peabody Conservatory Orchestra (1952–55). Assistant Conductor, London Philharmonic Orchestra (1955–57). Associate, then Principal Conductor, BBC Northern Symphony Orchestra (1958–68). Artistic Adviser, Western Orchestral Society (1969–73).

INBAL, Eliahu, b. 1936, Jerusalem, Israel. Also violinist. Chief Conductor, Frankfurt Symphony Orchestra (1974–) and a regular guest conductor in many countries since winning Guido Cantelli International Competition for Conductors (1963).

IRVING, Robert, b. 1913, Winchester, England. Musical Director, Sadler's Wells Royal Ballet (1949–58). Musical Director, New York City Ballet (1958–). His reputation as a ballet conductor is very high.

ITURBI, José, b. 1895, Valencia, Spain; d. Los Angeles, 1980. Also a famous pianist and a composer, combining conducting and playing at times. After making his name in Europe, made US debut (1929). Musical Director, Rochester Philharmonic Orchestra (1935–43). Permanent Conductor, Valencia Orchestra. Conducted leading orchestras all over the world, and appeared in films.

JACQUES, Reginald, b. 1894, Ashby-de-la-Zouche, England; d. Oxford, 1969. A leading choral and orchestral conductor. Founded the Jacques String Orchestra (1947).

JANIGRO, Antonio, b. 1918, Milan, Italy. Also a cellist. Founder/ Conductor of I Solisti dei Zagreb (1954–67) and has held important posts in Italy and Germany.

JÄRNEFELT, Armas, b. 1869, Viipuri, Finland; d. Stockholm, 1958. Also composer, best known for his 'Praeludium'. This Swedish conductor was at the Stockholm Opera (1905–06: 1907–32) and Helsinki Opera (1932–36).

JEHIN, Léon, b. 1853, Spa, Belgium; d. Monte Carlo, 1928. La Monnaie, Brussels (1882–88). Paris Opéra (1889–93), also conducting at Covent Garden (1891–92). The rest of his career was mainly at Monte Carlo.

JOCHUM, Eugen, b. 1902, Babenhausen, Germany. After his debut with the Munich Philharmonic Orchestra (1926), he was with various opera houses. Guest Conductor, Berlin Philharmonic (1932–). General-musikdirektor, Duisburg (1930–32) and

Eugen Jochum, a senior German conductor renowned for his performances of German and Austrian music.

Hamburg (1934–35). He has been a guest conductor around the world. Founder and Chief Conductor, Bavarian Radio Orchestra (1960). Has conducted at the leading festivals, including Bayreuth (1953–54: 1971–73). Conductor Laureate, London Symphony Orchestra (1975–79). His brother Georg Jochum (1909–70) was also a conductor, including Generalmusikdirektor, Linz (1940–45).

JONES, Geraint, b. 1917, Porth, Wales. Also an organist and harpsichordist. Founded the Geraint Jones Singers and Orchestra (1951). Regularly appears at the Proms, in Europe and the USA.

JORDA, Enrique, b. 1911, San Sebastian, Spain. Conductor, Madrid Symphony (1940–45). Cape Town Symphony Orchestra (1948–54). San Francisco Symphony Orchestra (1954–63). Many guest appearances. In San Francisco, he had the misfortune to fall foul of a typically cruel attack by George Szell.

JORDANS, Hein, b. 1914, Venlo, Holland. A leading Dutch conductor, whose posts include First Conductor, Het Brabants Orkest.

JORDANS, Weike, b. 1922, Venlo, Holland. Since his debut (1947) has conducted widely in Holland, also abroad, including Mozarteum Orchestra, Salzburg.

JØRGENSEN, Poul, b. 1934, Copenhagen, Denmark. Also a musicologist. Assistant Permanent Conductor, Royal Opera, Copenhagen. Royal Conductor (1964). Has conducted many European orchestras.

JULLIEN, Louis, b. 1812, Sisteron, France; d. Paris, 1860. This celebrated and flamboyant figure was 'the first of the important virtuoso-showman kind of conductor' (Harold Schonberg). His particular showplace was Britain: he directed Promenade Concerts of light music (1840–60) in London, the classics appearing from time to time – Mozart and Beethoven, suitably 'improved'. He also directed opera, including the 1847 Drury Lane season of English operas which was a disaster. Preferring vast orchestras, he believed in choirs of 1000 for oratorios. A great popularizer of music (though anathema to other musicians), he visited the USA (1853), complete with his monster quadrilles. He looked forward to setting the Lord's Prayer to music and the advertisement, 'words by Jesus Christ, music by Jullien'. Finally, he went mad.

KABALEWSKI, Wladyslaw, b. 1919, Warsaw, Poland. Also composer and violinist. Musical Director and Principal Conductor, Chamber Opera Society at State National Philharmonic (1963–65). State Musical Theatre and Operetta, Lublin (1965–71). Conducting Professor and Conductor, Symphony Orchestra, Warsaw Academy of Music (1966–).

KALINNIKOF, Vassili, b. 1866, Orel, Russia; d. Yalta, 1901. Also composer. Conductor of Italian opera, Marynskaya Theatre, St. Petersburg (1893).

KAMU, Okko, b. 1946, Helsinki, Finland. Also composer and violinist. With Finnish National Opera (1966–69). Winner of 1969 Karajan competition for conductors. Guest Conductor, Royal Swedish Opera (1969–70). Conductor, then Chief Conductor, Radio Symphony Orchestra, Finland (1970–77). Chief Conductor, and Music Director, Oslo Philharmonic (1975–79).

KARAJAN, Herbert von, b. 1908, Austria. Also a producer. First a brief outline of his rocket-like rise to his present enormous prestige and power: Debut: Salzburg, Landestheater (1927). Ulm (1927–34). Aachen (1934–38). Berlin State Opera (1938–45). Since 1945, many concert tours of Europe, America and the Far East. He has conducted regularly at La Scala, Milan (1948–). Artistic Director of the Salzburg Festival (1958–60: 1964–). Established the Salzburg Easter Festival (1963–), and is its Musical and Artistic Director. Artistic Director, Berlin Philharmonic Orchestra (1955–), Artistic Director, Vienna State Opera (1956–64). He made his name in Britain in the late '40s with the Philharmonia.

Karajan's breadth of musical sympathies is remarkable: he is renowned as a great conductor of Beethoven and Wagner, Strauss, Puccini and Mascagni etc., etc. Very much a technical, gadget-minded man of our time, he revels in recording techniques, acoustics, television, films and modern staging methods. He is known as the ringmaster of the Karajan Circus, and his life-style, musical and otherwise, is always news. Greatly admired, if not necessarily loved by his musicians, he has seen to it that the Berlin Philharmonic Orchestra is the best paid in the world. Arguments may continue about his high velocity performances of the classical repertoire, but there are none over his mastery of his profession and his powers of leadership. Beauty of orchestral sound is a hallmark of his conducting – a typical example is his *Tristan and Isolde* recording with the Berlin Philharmonic – though some have found a lack of dramatic meaning in his interpretations, for all their dramatic flair. He has made a number of musical films, including *Carmen*, *Otello* (his legendary Salzburg production), and Beethoven's Ninth Symphony, but his supreme ambition is a filming of the *Ring*. If it is ever achieved, it would be the ultimate climax to the career of the most truly Renaissance Man among present day conductors.

Karajan is not one for excessive movements. He will gracefully gesture with his arms, while his eyes, surprisingly, are closed. He achieves his dynamic readings while apparently relaxed yet his control is total. As has been noted elsewhere, his extreme admirers simply state that he is the world's greatest conductor. Such overstatement irritates, yet at least he is a worthy candidate.

KARASEK, Jiri, b. 1925, Brno, Czechoslovakia. State Theatre, Brno (1950–56: 1960–   ). JK Tyl Theatre, Pizen (1956–62). Stibor Theatre, Olomouc (1962–66) etc.

KASLIK, Václav, b. 1917, Policna, Czechoslovakia. Also producer, and composer. Musical Director, Brno (1943–45). Chief of Opera Ensemble, Theatre of May 5, Prague (1945–48).

Conductor, Smetana Theatre, Prague (1952–62). Chief Producer, National Theatre (1948–   ). He has conducted in Russia, Austria, Germany etc. and produced at La Scala, Covent Garden and other opera houses, often with the designer, Josef Svoboda.

KATAJA, Lassi, b. 1940, Ilmajoki, Finland. Also a composer. A well-known conductor in his own country. In charge of Rovaniemi Orchestra (1975–   ).

KATLEWICZ, Jerzy, b. 1927, Bochnia, Poland. After posts in Cracow and Poznan, he became Director, First Conductor and Artistic Director, National Cracow Philharmonia of Karol Szymanowski (1968–   ).

KEEFFE, Bernard, b. 1925, London, England. A busy conductor whose ability and personality as a speaker make him an ideal lecturer on music and opera on TV and radio.

KEILBERTH, Joseph, b. 1908, Karlsruhe, Germany; d. Munich, 1968. Generalmusikdirektor, Karlsruhe (1935–40). Conductor, Dresden (1945–50). Generalmusikdirektor, Munich (1959–68). At Bayreuth (1952–56). Particularly noted for his Strauss. Died conducting *Tristan und Isolde*.

KEMPE, Rudolf, b. 1910, Niederpoyritz, Germany; d. Zurich, Switzerland, 1976. Originally an oboist with Leipzig Gewandhaus Orchestra (1929–36). Conducting debut with Leipzig Opera (1935). At Chemnitz (1942–48). Weimar (1948–49), then

Rudolf Kempe, much admired by British players and a finer conductor than some more charismatic figures.

became Generalmusikdirektor at Dresden (1948–52). Munich (1952–54) and regularly at Covent Garden (1953–). Metropolitan, New York (1954–58). Principal Conductor, Royal Philharmonic Orchestra (1961–76). A wonderful trainer of orchestras – his British players adored him – he was famous for his Wagner and Strauss and, unlike many German conductors, for his Verdi and Puccini. However, some regarded his *Ring* as too much like Chamber music.

KERTÉSZ, Istvan, b. 1929, Budapest, Hungary; d. nr. Tel-Aviv, 1973. His early death came when his reputation in opera and symphonic music was very high. Debut, Budapest Opera (1954). Augsburg (1958–63). Cologne (1964–73), also conducting at Covent Garden. Principal Conductor, London Symphony Orchestra (1964–68). A famous Mozartian, who also gave remarkable performances of a number of modern operas, including Britten's *Billy Budd* and Prokofiev's *The Fiery Angel.*

KES, Willem, b. 1856, Dordrecht, Holland; d. Munich, Germany, 1934. Also a violinist. Original Conductor of the Concertgebouw Orchestra of Amsterdam (1888–95).

KETCHAM, Charles, b. 1942, San Diego, California. Assistant Conductor, Gulbenkian Orchestra, Lisbon (1970–73). Conductor, San Diego Symphony Orchestra (1973) and a guest conductor in many countries.

KLECKI (Kletzki), Paul, b. 1900, Lodz, Poland. Also composer. Principal Conductor, Kharkov Philharmonic Orchestra (1937). Director, Lucerne Festival (1944–45). Musical Director, Suisse Romande Orchestra (1967). Also a guest conductor in Europe, America, Israel and Australia.

KLEE, Bernhard, b. 1936, Leipzig, Germany. After posts in Cologne, Berne, Salzburg and Hanover, he became Generalmusikdirektor in Lubeck. Currently Chief Conductor, Dusseldorf Symphony Orchestra and Conductor, Norddeutscher Rundfunk Symphony Orchestra (1979), and a regular guest conductor in many countries. A regular visitor to Britain from the early '70s, appearing with leading orchestras in England and Scotland. First appeared at Covent Garden in *Così fan tutte* (1973).

KLEIBER, Carlos, b. 1930, Berlin, Germany. The son of Erich Kleiber (below), he has reached the level of his father's great talent, combining it with a perfectionism which requires particularly long rehearsals. After working in Argentina, where he had studied, he was at the Gärtnerplatz, Munich (1954–56) and the Vienna Volksoper (1956–58). Dusseldorf Opera (1958–64), Stuttgart Opera (1966–). National Theatre, Munich (1968–). He has also conducted at Bayreuth, Edinburgh Festival, Covent Garden, La Scala, etc. His *Otello* at Covent Garden (1980) is already legendary.

KLEIBER, Erich, b. 1890, Vienna, Austria; d. Zurich, Switzerland, 1956. One of the great conductors of the century, he held posts at Darmstadt (1912–18), Wuppertal (1919–21) and Mannheim (1922–23) before becoming Generalmusikdirektor of the Berlin State Opera (1923–34). His time in Berlin was one of the utmost brilliance. His world premières included *Wozzeck* (1925) after thirty-four full orchestral rehearsals. Though not a Jew, he resigned because of Nazi opposition to Hindemith's *Mathis der Maler* and went abroad as a guest conductor of concerts and opera. He had been a regular guest conductor of the Berlin Philharmonic (from 1924). He conducted in Italy, Britain and North and South America, most notably at the Teatro Colon, Buenos Aires (1937–49). He conducted the Concertgebouw Orchestra, Amsterdam (1933–38). Having made his name at Covent Garden (1938) with *Fliegende Holländer* and *Rosenkavalier*, he returned (1950–53) to the still new

opera company and raised its morale from near the depths. Orchestral and singing standards soared under him in *Rosenkavalier*, *Wozzeck* etc. His work in Buenos Aires, which he had first visited in 1926, was phenomenally successful in the opera house and concert hall, so masterly an orchestral trainer was he. He even transformed local orchestras in Chile, Peru, Mexico and elsewhere in Central and South America, finally doing the same inspired pioneer work in Cuba. Meanwhile, his German seasons at the Teatro Colon remain a legend.

Kleiber conducted in the USA, but not often: New York Philharmonic (1930–33), NBC Symphony (1947–48), as a guest conductor. He returned to Europe (1948) making a deep impression in London with the London Philharmonic Orchestra before his famous period at the Covent Garden. In 1954, he returned to the Berlin State Opera, only to find Communist interference odious. He then refused to conduct in West Germany as the West Germans had not allowed him to conduct while he was in East Germany. So, prickly to the end, and beloved by orchestral musicians the world over, he died in exile in Switzerland.

KLEIN, Kenneth, b. 1939, Los Angeles, California, USA. Musical Director, Guadalajara Symphony Orchestra (1961–). Invited by Casals to conduct Puerto Rico Symphony Orchestra (1973/74) and opened Festival Casals (1977). Has conducted many leading orchestras abroad, also opera at the Metropolitan, New York.

Founder of the Westside Symphony Orchestra (1963).

KLEMPERER, Otto, b. 1885, Breslau, Germany; d. Zurich, Switzerland, 1973. Also a composer and producer. Remembered, especially in Britain, for his magisterial Beethoven performances in his Olympian old age – despite being afflicted by accidents and disasters that would have crushed a lesser man – Klemperer's career was far more wide-ranging musically than that of many great modern conductors. After his debut in Berlin (1906), he was recommended to the German Theatre, Prague, by Mahler (1907–10). Then, from 1911–27, at Hamburg, Barmen, Strasbourg, Cologne and Wiesbaden. Kroll Opera, Berlin then at State Opera (1927–33), being forced to leave (as a Jew) by the Nazis.

Klemperer's repertory in Berlin was enormous. As well as operas in the standard repertory, his premières included *Cardillac*, *Neues vom Tage*, *Erwartung* and *From the House of the Dead*. After this extraordinary period, he settled in America, first as conductor of the Los Angeles Philharmonic (1933), guest conducting with the New York Philharmonic and (1937) reconstituting the Pittsburgh

Otto Klemperer, who in his Olympian old age seemed like Beethoven reborn to some of his worshippers.

Symphony Orchestra in six weeks. A tumour of the brain in 1939 ended his Los Angeles post. He had fallen in Leipzig in 1933, injuring his skull; now the tumour operation left him scarred and partially paralyzed. His temper, his bulk, his twisted scowling face, intensified the crisis and his career seemed virtually over. He was at the Budapest State Opera (1947–50), then came his extraordinary period of soaring fame in Britain with the Philharmonia Orchestra, becoming Musical Director (1955) and Conductor for Life (1959). Meanwhile, he had broken a femur in his leg (1951) and burnt himself badly in a smoking accident (1959), which caused the cancellation of his Metropolitan Opera debut with *Tristan*. In 1966 he broke a hip. By then he had begun to conduct (and produce) at Covent Garden, his finest achievement (naturally) being *Fidelio* (1961). *Lohengrin* and, especially, *The Magic Flute* were less well received, because of his over-deliberate tempos.

By now the more fanciful members of the British public, stirred to the depths by Klemperer's Beethoven performances, began to feel in his awesome presence that he was a reincarnation of the Master. He had become a US citizen, then an Israeli, but in these later years London knew him best – and worshipped him. There are recordings – of Beethoven, Brahms and Wagner – to prove that London was right.

KLINDWORTH, Karl, b. 1830, Hanover, Germany; d. Stolpe, Germany, 1916. Also a violinist and pianist: pupil of Liszt. Berlin Philharmonic Orchestra (1882–85). A friend of Wagner's, and an active propagandist for him in London (1854–68).

KLIPPSTATTER, Kurt, b. 1934, Graz, Austria. After various posts in Austria and Germany, he became Resident Conductor, Memphis Opera Theatre (1972) and Artistic Director (1974–).

KLOPFENSTEIN, René, b. 1927, Lausanne, Switzerland. After being a concert agent and Artistic Director, Philips Records, became a conductor. Concerts with Lamoureux Orchestra (1967). Director, Montreux-Vevey Music Festival, Switzerland (1968–), also guest appearances in Europe, Japan, South America, and Russia.

KNAPPERTSBUSCH, Hans, b. 1888, Elberfeld, Germany, d. Munich, Germany, 1965. Making his debut at Mulheim (1911), his early posts were at Bochum, Elberfeld, Leipzig and Dessau. He became General-musikdirektor of the Munich Opera (1922–36), but was forced to resign because of his anti-Nazi views, which he had openly aired. He had been Artistic Director of the Munich Festival (1923–35). Vienna State Opera (1936–50) and often conducted in Vienna until 1953. At Bayreuth (1951–64), where his performances of *The Ring* and *Parsifal* were widely revered. Indeed for many his *Parsifal* was incomparable: the noblest they had heard. He went back to Munich in 1954, also conducting in Paris, Rome, Zurich and Milan and once at Covent Garden (*Salome*, 1937). He was famous for his performances of Brahms and

Strauss, as well as his Wagner, also for his slow tempos and lack of enthusiasm for too many rehearsals, which made his players like him even more. When conductors started imitating Toscanini and conducting without the score, Knappertsbusch continued using one. When asked why, he said: 'Why not? I can read music.'

KNOCH, Ernst, b. 1875, Karlsruhe, Germany; d. New York, 1959. Assistant to Mottl at Karlsruhe (1898–1901), then at Strasbourg (1901–07), Essen (1907–09) and Cologne (1909–12). At Bayreuth (1904–07). Joined the Quinlan Company, with whom he conducted the first Australian *Tristan und Isolde* (1912). After conducting touring companies in the USA, he taught there from 1938.

KOLBE, Grethe, b. 1910, Kobenhavn, Denmark. Staff Conductor, Denmark Radio Concert Orchestra (1951–) and has been a guest conductor with leading European broadcasting companies and festivals of light music.

KONDRASHIN, Kirill, b. 1914, Moscow, Russia. Assistant Conductor, Nemirovich-Danchenko Musical Theatre, Moscow (1934–37). Maly Theatre Leningrad (1938–42). Bolshoi, Moscow (1943–56). All-Russia Symphony Orchestra Touring Concert Company (1956–60). Chief Conductor, Moscow Philharmonic Orchestra (1960). During the 1978–79 season at the Concertgebouw, Amsterdam, he became Conductor, having been Principal Guest Conductor, and asked for a Dutch residence permit to have

Kirill Kondrashin, now Conductor of the Concertgebouw of Amsterdam after a long career in Russia.

more control over his artistic life. Regularly conducts in Britain.

KONWITSCNY, Franz, b. 1901, Fulnek, Germany; d. Belgrade, Yugoslavia, 1962. Began as a violinist and violist. Stuttgart Opera (1926–33). Freiburg (1933–37). Frankfurt (1937–45). Hanover (1945–46). Leipzig Gewandhaus Orchestra (1949–53). Dresden (1953–56). He was selected as Generalmusikdirektor of the rebuilt Berlin State Opera (1955) on Kleiber's resignation. He conducted Covent Garden's *Ring* (1959), and also in Italy and eastern Europe. At his best in Mozart, Strauss, Wagner and Russian works.

KOSLER, Zdenék, b. 1928, Praha, Czechoslovakia. This leading Czech conductor has been mainly based in his homeland in opera and the concert hall. Prague Symphony Orchestra (1966). Czech Philharmonic Orchestra, Prague (1971–79). Chief Conductor, Opera of Slovak National Theatre, Bratislava (1971–). Became Musical Director, Prague Opera (1980–).

KOUSSEVITZKY, Serge, b. 1874, Vishny Volochek; d. Boston, Mass.,USA, 1951. He first made his name as a double-bass virtuoso before becoming perhaps the greatest of all Russian conductors. He founded his own Symphony Orchestra (1910) which was greatly admired. Debussy was one of many to praise it and its conductor with his 'burning will to serve music'. He remained in Russia after the Revolution, becoming conductor of the State Symphony Orchestra (1917–20), which had been the Imperial Orchestra. However, his frankness led him into trouble, though so great was his popularity that he survived, until he left for a year and never returned. Reaching Paris via Berlin, he founded the Concerts Koussevitzky (1921), then went to Boston (1924) to replace Pierre Monteux as Conductor of the Boston Symphony Orchestra. In Paris, as well as introducing much Russian symphonic music, he had given Russian opera (1921), also presenting a Russian season in Barcelona the same year. He conducted the Berlin Philharmonic Orchestra and the London Symphony Orchestra during this period.

In Boston he got off to a difficult start. A rich man, he was a self-taught conductor, his technique at that time was deficient, while his foul temper and rudeness made him hated, more so when he demanded many resignations at the end of his first season. The orchestra may not have been perfect, but neither was he. Gradually, things improved. His mania for perfectionism was respected, and conductor and orchestra, unhappily married, reached such heights that they were without equal in the USA, some would say by the early '40s, in the world. Koussevitzky continued to conduct in Paris until 1929. He was a champion of American music and made the Berkshire Music Festival, which he took over in 1937, the most important in the country. From his conducting class came Leonard Bernstein. His tastes were very wide and it was he who commissioned Britten's *Peter Grimes*. Particular favourites of his were *La Mer*, *Daphnis and Chloe*, Strauss's tone poems and Tchaikovsky's most famous symphonies. Guest conductors were rarely allowed in Boston, and comparatively few soloists appeared. He became an American citizen in 1941. No foreign conductor has served America better.

KOVAŘOVIC, Karel, b. 1862, Prague, Czechoslovakia; d. Prague, 1920. Also a composer. After posts at Brno and Pizen, he became Conductor of the Prague National Theatre (1900–20), where his services to Czech opera were immense. His repertory of non-Czech music was very wide and he greatly improved the company's standards.

KRAUSS, Clemens, b. 1893, Vienna; d. Mexico, 1954. After his debut at

Brno (1913), he held posts at Riga, Nürnberg and Stettin, going next to Vienna (1922–24) as assistant to Franz Schalk. Director, Frankfurt Opera (1924–29), then at Vienna (1929–35), Berlin (1935–37) and at Munich as Generalmusikdirektor (1937–42). A noted Mozartian and a great Straussian and friend of the composer, his Strauss premières included *Arabella* (Dresden, 1933), *Friedenstag* (Munich, 1938), *Capriccio* (Munich, 1942 to his own libretto) and *Die Liebe der Danae* (Satzburg, 1952). He inspired devotion in his singers, some of whom followed him from Vienna to Berlin, then Dresden. They included Julius Patzak, Adele Kern and Viorica Ursuleac, who became his wife. Though a member of the Nazi party for ten years, he helped many refugees escape from Germany. He appeared at Covent Garden from 1934 when the first British *Arabella* was given with his wife in the title-role.

KRIPS, Henry, b. 1912, Vienna, Austria. Resident Conductor, South Australia Symphony Orchestra (1949–), with annual tours of Europe, including leading British orchestras.

KRIPS, Josef, b. 1902, Vienna, Austria; d. Geneva, Switzerland, 1974. A pupil of Weingartner, he held posts at Vienna (Volksoper, 1921), Dortmund (1925–26), Karlsruhe (1926–33), then at the Vienna State Opera (1933–38). until being driven out by the Nazis. He went to Belgrade, but could only work for a single season. Returning to Vienna after the war, which he was lucky to have survived, he conducted the first post-war opera performance at the Volksoper and was chiefly responsible for the Opera's rapid rebirth and splendour of achievement, especially in Mozart. He also helped reopen the Salzburg Festival (1946–50). After his Covent Garden debut with the Vienna State Opera (1947), he conducted the resident company (1963: 1971–74), also the Chicago Opera (1960), the Metropolitan, New York (1966–67: 1969–70), and performances in Amsterdam, Rome, Florence and Paris. Krips was Principal Conductor of the London Symphony Orchestra (1950–54) and the San Francisco Symphony Orchestra (1963–70). He was very highly regarded by musicians and public alike, though many of his players found him a tyrant.

KROMBHOLC, Jarolslav, b. 1918, Prague, Czechoslovakia. Guest Conductor, Prague National Theatre and Czech Philharmonic Orchestra (1940). Prague National Theatre (1949–68), becoming First Conductor. Head of Prague National Theatre Opera (1968) becoming Chief Conductor (1970). He has conducted widely in Europe, including Covent Garden and the English National Opera. Currently Chief Conductor, Prague Radio Symphony Orchestra.

KUBELIK, Rafael, b. 1914, Bychory, Bohemia. Also a composer. Son of the violinist, Jan Kubelik. Czech Philharmonic Society (1936–39). Musical Director, Brno Opera (1939–41). Czech Philharmonic Orchestra (1942–48). Chicago Symphony Orchestra (1950–53), where he was not popular with the tough critic of the *Daily Tribune* critic, Claudia Cassidy, a powerful local voice. Musical Director, Royal Opera House, Covent Garden (1955–58), a successful appointment which included the first British *Jenufa* and the historic *Les Troyens* (1957), or, more accurately, *The Trojans*. Not quite complete, it was a triumph and a landmark in Berliozian history. He also encouraged British singers. Bavarian Radio Symphony Orchestra (1961–   ). Musical Director of the Metropolitan, New York (1973–74), the Met.'s first, but resigned because of budget cuts. San Francisco Opera (1977). A very wide-ranging guest conductor in both concert hall and opera. English operagoers recall his Covent Garden period with affection, for it saw the transition towards a great international house. Currently (1980), Principal Conductor, Bavarian Radio Symphony Orchestra.

KURTZ, Efrem, b. 1900, St. Petersburg, Russia. Berlin Philharmonic Orchestra (1921–33). Musical Director, Stuttgart Philharmonic Orchestra (1924–33) and many guest appearances, especially in USA, of which he is now a citizen. Has conducted in Australia, Japan and Israel, and all over Europe. Regularly conducts the Hallé Orchestra (1973–   ).

LA MARCHINA, Robert, b. 1928, New York City, USA. Also a cellist. His posts include Music Director and Conductor, Metropolitan Opera National Co. (1964–66), Honolulu Symphony Society and Hawaii Opera Theatre (1967–). He has also conducted at the Metropolitan, New York, Spoleto Festival, New York Philharmonic, Chicago Symphony and orchestras abroad.

LACHNER, Franz, b. 1803, Rain ober Lech, Germany; d. Munich, 1890. Also a composer. After conducting in Vienna (1826–34), Mannheim (1834–36), he went to Munich (1836), becoming Generalmusikdirektor (1852–90). It was he who made the Munich Opera world famous. Though originally anti-Wagner, he produced *Tannhauser* and *Lohengrin*, and, though not in sympathy with the new German music, had a wide-ranging repertory in Munich and an orchestra capable of rising to the demands of *Tristan und Isolde*. His brothers Ignaz (1807–95) and Vincenz (1811–93) were also successful conductors.

LAMBERT, Constant, b. 1905, London, England; d. London, 1951. Also a composer. This brilliant all-round musician's most remarkable contribution was to ballet. With Ninette de Valois and Frederick Ashton, he was one of the architects of the Sadler's Wells (later Royal) Ballet, being Musical Director of the Vic-Wells and Sadler's Wells Ballet (1932) and, finally, Music Adviser (1948). He also conducted leading symphony orchestras and opera.

LAMOUREUX, Charles, b. 1834, Bordeaux, France; d. Paris, 1899. Also a violinist. An early French Wagnerian, he was at the Opéra Comique (1876–77) and the Opéra (1877–79). Organized the Lamoureux Concerts (from 1881), which included long pieces of Wagner. He did much to popularize French music in Britain.

LANCHBERY, John, b. 1923, London, England. A ballet specialist, much of his career (from 1951) has been with the Sadler's Wells/Royal Ballet. Principal Conductor (1960–72), since when he has been Musical Director of Australian Ballet. Also an arranger of ballet music, most notably, *La Fille mal gardée*.

LANKESTER, Michael, b. 1944, London, England. Also a composer.

Musical Director, National Theatre (1969–75). Conductor, Surrey Philharmonic Orchestra (1972–   ) and a guest conductor with other orchestras.

LASSEN, Eduard, b. 1830, Copenhagen, Denmark; d. Weimar, Germany, 1904. Also a composer. He succeeded Liszt at Weimar (1859–94).

LAWRENCE, Ashley, b. 1934, Hamilton, New Zealand. Touring Royal Ballet (1962–66). Conductor Berlin Opera Ballet (1966–72). Stuttgart Ballet (1970–72). Rejoining Royal Ballet (1972), he became Musical Director (1973). Principal Conductor, BBC Concert Orchestra (1971–   ).

LAZAR, Joel, b. 1941, New York City, USA. Teacher and conductor at Harvard (1959–71). New York University (1966–69). University of Virginia (1969–71), giving many local premières. Has conducted in Britain, Denmark. Assistant to Horenstein (1971–73).

LEDGER, Philip, b. 1937, Bexhill-on-Sea, England. Posts include Artistic Director, Aldeburgh Festival (1968) and Director of Music and Organist, King's College, Cambridge (1974–   ). A brilliant harpsichordist.

LEHEL, Gyorgy, b. 1926, Budapest, Hungary. Musical Director and Chief Conductor, Budapest Symphony Orchestra (of Hungarian Radio and TV) since 1962. He has conducted all over Europe, in North America and in Japan.

LEINSDORF, Erich, b. 1912, Vienna, Austria. Assistant at Salzburg to Bruno Walter (1934) and Toscanini (1935–37). He went to the Metropolitan, New York (1938), taking over from Bodansky as Chief Conductor, German repertory (1939–43). He went back to the Met. as Musical Consultant (1958–62) and as a guest conductor (1971–   ). Cleveland Orchestra (1943–46), then with the Rochester Philharmonic. He was Musical and Artistic Director of the New York City Opera (1956–57) and with San Francisco Opera (1938–41: 1948: 1951: 1955: 1957) and conducted *Meistersinger* at Bayreuth (1959). He became Musical Director of the Boston Symphony Orchestra (1962–69), and though some found his approach too clinical, his technical prowess and dedication was never in doubt. Though his approach to Italian opera has been sometimes considered inflexible, there is a *Ballo in Maschera* recording of his which is unequalled. He has conducted most of the world's leading orchestras.

LEITNER, Ferdinand, b. 1912, Berlin, Germany. Debut, Berlin (1943), though he had previously been Busch's assistant at Glyndebourne (1935). Hamburg Opera (1945–46). Munich (1946–47). Musical Director, Stuttgart (1947–69) since when he has been Musical Director, Zurich Opera. He has conducted major orchestras in Europe, Asia, Australia and N. and S. America.

LEONHARDT, Gustav, b. 1928, Graveland, Holland. Also a harpsichordist and organist. An expert in baroque music.

LEPPARD, Raymond, b. 1927, London, England. Also a musicologist, who has led the Monteverdi and Cavalli revival in Britain, realizing operas as well as conducting them, from the historic *L'Incoronazione di Poppea* (Glynde-bourne, 1962) onwards. His realiz-ations have been condemned for lack of authenticity by some who consider them too richly lush, but Monteverdi especially is now widely loved because of him. Principal Conductor, BBC Northern Symphony Orchestra (1973–). He has conducted opera at Glyndebourne, Aldeburgh, Santa Fé, Covent Garden, English National Opera, Drottingholm, etc. Chief Guest Conductor, Scottish Chamber Orchestra.

LEVI, Hermann, b. 1839, Giessen, Germany; d. Munich, 1900. This great operatic conductor was at Saarbrucken (1859–61), Rotterdam (1861–64) and Karlsruhe (1864–72) before becoming Principal Conductor at Munich (1872–96). First anti-Wagnerite, he became a Wagnerian, so losing his friendship with Brahms. The anti-Semitic Wagner – Levi was a rabbi's son – admired and liked him though he strained the friendship by suggesting Levi should be baptized before conducting *Parsifal*! Despite this and other gaffes, Levi conducted the première (1882), which was a personal triumph for him. He conducted at Wagner's funeral (1883). At his best, a superb and inspirational conductor, though he could be pedestrian. He was a champion of Mozart's operas preparing new versions, which helped popularize the composer, though now his versions are naturally forgotten.

LEVINE, James, b. 1943, Cincinnatti, Ohio, USA. Assistant to George Szell at Cleveland (1964–70). At the Metropolitan, New York (1971–), becoming Principal Conductor (1972) and Musical Director (1975–). Salzburg (1976–). Perhaps the most gifted American conductor of his generation, his success at the Metropolitan has been universally recognized. His range is considerable: Wagner and Verdi, Mozart and Britten. His Salzburg triumphs have included *La Clemenza di Tito* and *Der Zauberflöte*, while his revitalization of the orchestra of the Metropolitan has made it at its best the equal of any opera orchestra in the world. A 1980 triumph for conductor and orchestra was a magnificent *Wozzeck*.

LEWIS, (Sir) Anthony, b. 1915, Bermuda. Also composer and Principal, Royal Academy of Music (1968–). A notable conductor of 17th and 18th century music, of which he has made many recordings. Knighted in 1972.

LEWIS, Henry, b. 1932, Los Angeles, California, USA. Began as a double-bass player. Conductor, Los Angeles Philharmonic Orchestra (1961–65). He has conducted concerts and opera widely in America, Britain and at La Scala, including performances with his wife, the distinguished mezzo, Marilyn Horne. Conductor, New Jersey Symphony Orchestra (1968) at the Metropolitan, New York, also guest appearances with leading British orchestras, at La Scala and elsewhere.

LINDARS, Herman, b. 1899, Reading, England. Also composer. Has conducted leading British orchestras, including the Hallé. Toured Russia with Sir Malcolm Sargent and the Royal Philharmonic (1963).

LISZT, Franz, b. 1811, Raiding, Hungary; d. Bayreuth, 1886. The great composer and pianist and patron of music was also a notable conductor. As Kapellmeister at Weimar (1848–58) he conducted the first *Lohengrin* (1850) and the revised *Benvenuto Cellini* (1852) also *Der Barbier von Bagdad* (1858).

LLOYD-JONES, David, b. 1934, London, England. His career has been mainly operatic, with the English National Opera, Covent Garden, Scottish Opera, Welsh National Opera. Has also conducted many leading British orchestras. Especially noted for his performances of Russian operas. Principal Conductor, English National Opera North (1978–).

LOCKHART, James, b. 1930, Edinburgh, Scotland. Assistant Conductor, Yorkshire Symphony Orchestra (1954–55). Assistant Conductor, Münster City Opera (1955–56). Bavarian State Opera (1956–57). Glyndebourne Festival Opera (1957–59). At Covent Garden (1959–60), also conducted Sadler's

James Levine is, for many, the most gifted American conductor of his generation.

Wells Opera and Scottish Opera. He became Music Director, Welsh National Opera (1968–72), then Generalmusikdirektor, Kassel Opera (1972–), the first British-born conductor to hold such a post in a German opera house. He has conducted widely in Germany, both concerts and opera, also in Italy, and has been a guest conductor with most leading British orchestras.

LOMBARD, Alain, b. 1940, Paris, France. Has conducted concerts and opera in France, Austria, Germany and the USA. Musical Director, Strasbourg Orchestre Philharmonique (1980) and Opera du Rhin.

LOPEZ COBOS, Jesus, b. 1940, Toro, Spain. Debut, Prague (1968), since when he has conducted in many countries, notably the Concertgebouw of Amsterdam and the London Symphony Orchestra.

LOUGHRAN, James, b. 1931, Glasgow, Scotland. Associate Conductor, Bournemouth Symphony Orchestra (1962–65). Principal Conductor, BBC Scottish Orchestra (1965–71). Principal Conductor and Musical Adviser, Hallé Orchestra (1971–), also Conductor, Bamberg Symphony Orchestra. Currently recording all the Beethoven symphonies with the Hallé to considerable critical acclaim. He

conducted the First and Last Nights of the 1979 Proms.

LOVETT, Leon, b. 1935. Since his debut at Sadler's Wells (*Traviata*, 1958), he has worked widely at home and abroad in opera and concerts, conducting more than twenty British premières of operas, including Henze's *Boulevard Solitude* for the New Opera Company and Szymanowski's *King Roger* and Shostakovich's *The Nose* for English National Opera. Musical Director, London Choral Society (1973) and London Oriana Choir (1974). Formed English Baroque Orchestra and Choir.

LUBBOCK, John, b. 1945, Much Hadham, England. Founder-Conductor, Orchestra of St. John's, Smith Square, London.

LUDWIG, Leopold, b. 1908, Ostrava-Vitkovice, Austria. Posts have included Vienna (1939–43), Berlin State Opera (1943–50) and Generalmusikdirektor, Hamburg State Opera (1950–71). His many guest appearances have included San Francisco Opera (1958–68).

LULLY, Jean Baptiste, b. 1632, Florence, Italy; d. Paris, 1687. Louis XIV's master of music. As well as composing, he was in charge of a notable string orchestra. See Chapter 1.

M

MAAG, Peter, b. 1919, St. Gallen, Switzerland. Also a pianist. Dusseldorf Opera (1952–54). Musical Director, Bonn Opera (1954–59). Chief Conductor, Vienna Volksoper (1964–67). He has also appeared at various Italian opera houses, including Parma. Musical Director, Turin (1974–76). At Covent Garden (1958: 1977) and Chicago (1961). New York, Metropolitan (1974–). Particularly fine in Mozart.

MAAZEL, Lorin, b. 1930, Neuilly, France. A child prodigy who was invited by Toscanini to conduct the NBC Orchestra. After studying in Europe and the USA, this American conductor's career has included Bayreuth (1960: 1968–69) and Artistic Director, Deutsche Oper Berlin (1965–71), Metropolitan, New York (1962) and Covent Garden, *Luisa Miller* (1978–79). Music Director, Berlin Radio Symphony Orchestra (1965). He has conducted at La Scala, Milan, and the Vienna State Opera (Director designate, 1982–86). Music Director, Cleveland Orchestra (1972–). Associate Principal Conductor, New Philharmonia Orchestra (1971–1976) Principal Guest Conductor (1976–80). A guest conductor with many of the world's leading orchestras. Conducted the Philharmonia in London's first Mahler cycle (1979). Chief Guest Conductor, Orchestre National de France.

MACAL, Zdenek, b. 1936, Brno, Czechoslovakia. After becoming

Lorin Maazel, once a child prodigy, now internationally famous in both concert hall and opera house.

Principal Conductor, Prague Symphony Orchestra and winning major conducting competitions, he had a great success conducting the Czech Philharmonic at home and on tour. Generalmusikdirektor, Cologne Radio Symphony Orchestra (1970–74). American debut with the Chicago Symphony Orchestra (1972). Two major tours with the Hamburg Radio Orchestra (1978–79) and many guest appearances with major British, German and other orchestras (1979–).

MACKERRAS, (Sir) Charles, b. Schenectady, New York, USA. One of the best all-round opera conductors in the world. An Australian, he was principal oboist of the Australian Symphony Orchestra (1943–46). Sadler's Wells Opera (1948–53) after which he was Principal Conductor BBC Concert Orchestra (1954–56). First Conductor, Hamburg State Opera (1966–70), Sadler's Wells (1963–) becoming Musical Director, English National Opera (1970–77); a most distinguished period. He has been a guest conductor of many British and European orchestras. He has done more than anyone else to promote the cause of Janáček in Britain, including the first British performances of *Kátá Kabanová* (1951), and *The Makropoulos Case* (1964) and the English première of *From the House of the Dead*, (1965) all at Sadler's Wells. Other premières have included Berkeley's *Ruth* (1956) and Britten's *Noyes Fludde* (1958), both for the English Opera Group. He has conducted at the Paris Opéra since 1973, while his *Pineapple Poll* ballet suite (from Sullivan's music) is perennially popular. Chief Guest Conductor, BBC Symphony Orchestra (1979). Knighted in 1977.

MACMILLAN, (Sir) Ernest, b. 1893, Mimico, Ontario, Canada. Conductor, Toronto Symphony Orchestra (1931–56) and Mendelssohn Choir (1942–57). He has also held major academic posts and has composed and written about music. One of the leading figures in Canadian musical life for many years. Knighted (1935).

MADERNA, Bruno, b. 1920, Venice, Italy; d. Darmstadt, Germany, 1973. Also a composer. Best known for his performances of modern opera, also of Monteverdi and Rameau. His premières included Nono's *Intolleranza* (Venice, 1960). Florence Festival (1964: 1970). Holland Festival (1965–68: 1973). He also conducted at La Scala, Milan, and in New York.

MADEY, Boguslaw, b. 1932, Sosnowiec, Poland. Also a composer and pianist. A leading figure in Warsaw and Lodz opera, also as a teacher of conducting, he has conducted widely outside Poland. Guest Conductor, Deutsche Oper am Rhein, Dusseldorf (1973).

MAHLER, Gustav, b. 1860, Kalist, Bohemia; d. Vienna, 1911. The great composer was also a great conductor (as noted in Chapter 1). After working at Ljubljana, Olomouc, Kassel, Prague, Leipzig and Budapest (1881–91), he was at Hamburg (1891–97) and, most notably, at the Vienna State Opera (1897–1907), being appointed Director in July, 1897.

There is no doubt that his genius and demand for perfectionism in every department, raised the Vienna Opera to heights unequalled then and (except in stage techniques) since. Yet he was an autocrat, and was cordially disliked by his players, and hired and fired at will, often sacking an artist who had been extolled by him to the skies until found to have been a mere mortal. Wildly extravagant he may have been, but he cleared the Opera's deficit and was adored by young Vienna. 'Tradition is slovenliness' was his famous battlecry, and he went in for considerable editing of scores, heightened drama and sometimes startling rubatos.

Having made many enemies, he resigned because of administrative troubles and anti-Semitism, though some claim it was because his own music was not accepted. He had given London its first *Ring* cycle at Covent Garden (1892). Now, after the years of storm and glory in Vienna, he went to the Metropolitan, New York (1907–10). At first all went well, not least because the casts were unequalled, and, strangely, he allowed cuts, having allowed none in Vienna. He even accepted inferior settings. He was not a fit man, rivalry with Toscanini hardly helped, and there is no doubt that his work at the Metropolitan bore little comparison to the wonders of Vienna. His spell with the New York Philharmonic (1909–11) began with his changing two-thirds of the players, and steadily things got worse. The ladies of the Board actually 'tried' him for his alleged faults. By this time no one was in the right, Mahler included. He returned to Vienna to die.

Immortality was soon to be his as a composer, while because of his Vienna period he is immortal in the annals of opera. As for his days in New York, the misery of it was mainly brought about by his own character and state of health. It is a sorry story.

MALCOLM, George, b. 1917, London, England. Also a composer, harpsichordist and pianist. Master of Music, Westminster Cathedral (1947–59). Artistic Director, Philomusica of London (1962–66). During his remarkable period at Westminster Cathedral, Benjamin Britten wrote his *Missa Brevis* for the choir.

MALKO, Nikolai, b. 1883, Brailov, Russia; d. Sydney, Australia, 1961. Conductor, State Opera and Ballet, St. Petersburg (1908–18). Leningrad Philharmonic Orchestra (1927), also engagements in many European and American cities. Sydney Symphony Orchestra (1956–61).

MANCINELLI, Luigi, b. 1848, Orvieto, Italy; d. Rome, 1921. Also a composer. A cellist until he took over from a drunken conductor in *Aida* in Rome (1874). Chief Conductor, Drury Lane, London (1887) and at Covent Garden (1888–1905), giving the first English *Falstaff, Tosca* and *Werther*. Musical Director, Theatre Royal, Madrid (1888–95) also conducting in Italy and Portugal. At the Metropolitan, New York (1893–1903), conducting many local premières including *Falstaff, Bohème, Tosca* and *Die Zauberflöte*. He also conducted Wagner, more controversially, but with some German admirers. An outstanding conductor of the era just before Toscanini.

MANNS, (Sir) August, b. 1825, nr. Stettin, Germany; d. London, 1907. At first a military bandsman and composer of dance music. Conductor at London's Crystal Palace (1855–1901), where he was a great popularizer of symphonic music at low prices. Knighted (1903).

MARIANI, Angelo, b. 1821, Ravenna, Italy; d. Geneva, Switzerland, 1873. The first great modern Italian conductor. He gave the première of Verdi's *I Due Foscari* (1846), in Milan which greatly pleased the composer, who became a close friend. His performances of *Nabucco* and *I Lombardi* nearly landed him in jail for inciting rebellion, so thrilling were they, and, as well as many magnificent Verdi performances in Bologna, he also gave the Italian premières of *Lohengrin* (1871) and *Tannhäuser* (1872). His attitude to opera as an integrated theatrical art form was ahead of his time (except among composers who have invariably wanted it). Sadly, he fell out with Verdi because he refused to conduct the première of *Aida* in Cairo because of ill-health.

MARINUZZI, Gino, b. 1882, Palermo, Sicily; d. Milan, 1945. Also a composer. After posts in Italy and Sicily (including Palermo's first *Tristan* 1909), he was at the Teatro Colon, Buenos Aires, giving the first local *Parsifal* (1913). Later at Monte Carlo, then Chicago Opera (1919–21) and Rome Opera (1928–34). La Scala, Milan (1934–44).

MARK, Peter, b. 1940, New York City, USA. Boy soprano, then a violist. Artistic Director and Conductor, Vancouver Opera Association (1975–79). Artistic Director and Conductor, Virginia Opera Association (1975–), an astonishing success story, reaching a new peak of achievement with *Mary, Queen of Scots* (1977), the composer, Thea Musgrave, being the conductor's wife.

MARKEVITCH, Igor, b. 1912, Kiev, Russia. Also a composer. Originally a violinist and orchestra leader, he became a conductor in 1946, his posts including Musical Director, Symphony Orchestra of Montreal (1955–60). Permanent Conductor, Radio and TV Orchestra of Spain (1965). Became Artistic Director, Monte Carlo Orchestra and Opera (1968). A wide-ranging guest conductor.

MARRINER, Neville, b. 1924, Lincoln, England. Originally a violinist. Founder-Director of the Academy of St. Martin-in-the-Fields (1959), especially famous for performances of baroque string music. Conductor of the Los Angeles Chamber Orchestra (1969–77). Musical Director, Minnesota Orchestra (1979–).

MARSCHNER, Heinrich, b. 1795, Zittau, Saxony; d. Hanover, 1861. Also a composer. Musical Director, Dresden (1823–26). Kapellmeister, Leipzig (1827–31). Hoftheater,

Hanover (1830–61). His *Der Vampyr* and *Hans Heiling* are still given in Germany.

MARSICK, Armand, b. 1877, Liège, Belgium; d. Haine-saint-Paul, Brussels, 1959. Also a composer. Conductor, Athens Symphony Orchestra (1908–22). Bilbao (1922–27). Liège (1927–39). His father was the great violinist Martin Marsick.

MARTINON, Jean, b. 1910, Lyons, France; d. Paris 1976. Also a composer. Paris Conservatoire Orchestra (from 1944). Chicago Orchestra (1964–68). Paris National Orchestra (from 1968) etc. Residentir Orchestra, The Hague (1974). Many guest appearances abroad including London from 1946.

MARTUCCI, Giuseppe, b. 1856, Capua, Italy; d. Naples, 1909. Gave the first Italian *Tristan* (Bologna, 1888). Director of Conservatoire, Bologna (1886–1902) and Naples (1902–09).

MASCHERONI, Eduardo, b. 1852, Milan, Italy; d. Como, Italy, 1941. Also a composer. La Scala, Milan (1892–95), his premières including *La Wally*, also *Falstaff* at Verdi's request. He also gave the first La Scala *Tannhäuser*, *Fliegende Holländer* and *Die Walküre*. Later conducted in Germany, Spain and South America.

MASSON, Diego, b. 1935, France. A pupil of Boulez, he founded Musique Vivante (1966), conducting this contemporary music group on many occasions. He has conducted widely in France, including at the Aix and Avignon Festivals, and regularly at the Angers Opera. With Glyndebourne Touring Opera (1977) and has conducted leading British orchestras and the Concertgebouw of Amsterdam. Music Director, Marseilles Opera (1975–).

MASUR, Kurt, b. 1927, Silesia. This East German conductor became Generalmusikdirektor, Mecklenburg State Theatre (1958–1960), then worked with the producer Felsenstein at the Berlin Komischer Oper (1960–64). Chief Conductor, Dresden Philharmonic Orchestra (1967–70). Kapellmeister, Leipzig Gewandhaus Orchestra (1970–75). A notably dynamic conductor, he has appeared as a guest conductor with most of Europe's leading orchestras, also in the USA, Japan and South America. Principal Guest Conductor, Dallas Symphony Orchestra (1976–).

MATA, Eduardo, b. 1942, Mexico City, Mexico. Gave first performances in Mexico of music of the 1960s: Boulez, Stockhausen etc. Posts held in Mexico include Musical Director, Mexican Ballet Company (1963–64), Musical Director Guadalajara Symphony Orchestra (1965–66), also the National Symphony Orchestra of Mexico and Technical Director and Chief Conductor of the Pablo Casals Festival, Mexico (1976). He is now regarded as the foremost Mexican musician. His American posts include Principal Conductor, Phoenix Symphony Orchestra, then (1977–), Musical Director, Dallas Symphony Orchestra. Regular tours of Europe and the Far East. London debut with the London Symphony Orchestra

(1974), the year he first conducted the Berlin Philharmonic. He has toured Mexico with the London Symphony and the Philharmonia, also the Israel Philharmonic. Conducted the London Symphony Orchestra in six concerts for the British/Mexican Festival (1979).

MATAČIĆ, Lovro von, b. 1899, Susak, Yugoslavia. Conducted widely between the wars in Yugoslavia, including Zagreb Opera (1932–38). Vienna Volksoper (1942–45). Since 1954, he has conducted regularly in Germany and Italy. Generalmusik-direktor, Dresden (1956–58) while sharing the post in Berlin with Konwitschny. Succeeded Solti at Frankfurt (1961–66). Artistic Director, Monte Carlo (1974). He has also conducted in Munich, Bayreuth etc. and regularly produces operas. Musical Director, Zagreb Philharmonic Orchestra.

MAUCERI, John, b. 1945, New York City, USA. Has conducted at the Metropolitan, New York, also the Los Angeles Philharmonic, San Francisco Symphony etc., and in Vienna and Spoleto, where he conducted the première of Menotti's *Tamu-Tamu* (1974), also the West Coast première of *Death in Venice* (San Francisco, 1975). Has also conducted at Santa Fé Opera, Welsh National Opera etc. Musical Director, Washington Opera.

MAYER, Thomas, b. 1907, Germany. Leading West German conductor, whose posts have included Metropolitan, New York (1947) with Fritz Busch, then at the Teatro Colon, Buenos Aires with Erich Kleiber. Also with National Orchestra of Canada.

Regularly with Sinfonie Orchestra of West Berlin (1974–   ).

MEHTA, Zubin, b. 1936, Bombay, India. Now one of the leading conductors of the day, he studied conducting at the Vienna Musikakademie with Hans Swarowsky, making his debut in 1958. Won the International Conductors' Competition in Liverpool (1958) and had a year as the Assistant Conductor of the Royal Liverpool Philharmonic Orchestra. Music Director, Montreal Symphony Orchestra (1960–64) and in 1960 first conducted the Israel Philharmonic Orchestra, later

Born in India, Zubin Mehta won a conductors' competition in 1958, a portent of triumphs to come.

becoming its Music Adviser (1968–). Music Director, Los Angeles Philharmonic Orchestra (1961–76). In 1977, he became Music Director of the New York Philharmonic Orchestra, having meanwhile established himself as a brilliant operatic conductor as well. His operatic debuts include Florence (*Tosca*, 1965), Salzburg (*Die Entführung aus dem Serail*, 1965), Metropolitan, New York (*Aida*, 1965), La Scala, Milan (*Salome*, 1974) and Covent Garden (*Otello*, 1977). One of the finest Puccinians of the age, his *La Fanciulla del West* at Covent Garden (1977) helped 'make' the opera in Britain for everyone except the irredeemable.

MENDELSSOHN, Felix, b. 1809, Hamburg, Germany; d. Leipzig, 1847. The great composer was also one of the first great conductors, notably in Germany and Britain. See Chapters 1 and 3.

MENGELBERG, Willem, b. 1871, Utrecht, Holland; d. Zuort, Switzerland, 1951. Nicknamed the Napoleon of the Orchestra, this great virtuoso was in charge of the Concertgebouw of Amsterdam from 1895 to 1941. A famous conductor of the Romantic school, he excelled in Mahler and Strauss, who dedicated *Ein Heldenleben* to him. Regularly in the USA (from 1905). Conductor of the New York Philharmonic (1921–30), he also appeared in Britain (from 1911). His collaboration with the Nazis in World War Two forced him into exile after it. A romantic virtuoso conductor who excelled in orchestral colour, he was also a retoucher of scores and a great talker and raconteur at rehearsals.

MEROLA, Gaetano, b. 1881, Naples, Italy; d. San Francisco, USA, 1953. Much of his career was in the USA. Best remembered for his distinguished spell as Musical Director and Manager of the San Francisco Opera (1923–53) which he made America's second company after the Metropolitan. His roster of singers was as exciting as it was vast. He died conducting the San Francisco Symphony Orchestra in an open-air concert.

MEYLAN, Jean, b. 1915, Geneva, Switzerland, where he made his debut (1941). Chief Conductor, Radio Orchestra, Cologne (1949). Permanent Guest Conductor, Grand Theatre de Geneve (1962–), also many guest appearances elsewhere.

MITROPOULOS, Dimitri, b. 1896, Athens, Greece; d. Milan, 1960. Also a composer and pianist, he became a conductor in 1930. Minneapolis Symphony Orchestra (1937–49). New York Philharmonic Orchestra (1950–56). Metropolitan, New York (1954–60). Conducted at La Scala, Milan. A noted champion of modern music, including Berg and Schoenberg, also earlier giants including Strauss and Busoni (who had been his piano teacher). He used no baton and his jerky beat and physical gyrations were notorious, but his musicianship was wide-ranging and, as Harold Schonberg relates, he had a photographic memory. 'One glance at a score and it would be committed for good.' Alas, the other side of the coin was less of a blessing, though speaks volumes for his character. Much liked by his players, he was perhaps too goodnatured to enforce his will, and orchestral discipline suffered.

MOLINARI, Bernardino, b. 1880, Rome, Italy; d. Rome, 1952. Best remembered for his long association with the Augusteo concerts in Rome (from 1912), though he guest-conducted many concerts and opera in Europe and America.

MOLINARI-PRADELLI, Francesco, b. 1911, Bologna. Since 1942, he has conducted at leading Italian opera houses, also at Covent Garden (1955: 1960) and at San Francisco (1957–66) and Metropolitan, New York (1966–73) and Vienna (1959–   ).

MONTEUX, Pierre, b. 1875, Paris, France; d. Hancock, Maine, USA, 1964. First a violist. Concerts Berlioz (1910). Conductor for Diaghilev's Ballets Russe (1911–14), including the premières of *Petrouschka*, *Le Sacré du Printemps* (complete with the famous audience riot on the first night), and Ravel's *Daphnis and Chloe*. At the Metropolitan, New York (1917–19: 1953–56), where he gave many American premières including *The Golden Cockerel* (1918). Boston Symphony Orchestra (1919–24). Concertgebouw of Amsterdam (1924–34). He founded the Orchestre Symphonique de Paris (1928–38). Musical Director, San Francisco Symphony Orchestra (1936–52). He became Musical Director of the London Symphony Orchestra in 1961, aged eighty-six! Greatly liked by his players, he had a clear beat and was

one of the most motionless of conductors. He excelled in German as well as French music.

MONTGOMERY, Kenneth, b. 1943, Belfast, Northern Ireland. Debut, Glyndebourne (1967). Staff Conductor, Sadler's Wells Opera (1967–70). At Bournemouth (1973) as Assistant Conductor, Bournemouth Symphony Orchestra and Director, Bournemouth Sinfonietta. Musical Director, Glyndebourne Touring Opera (1974–76).

MORLACCHI, Francesco, b. 1784, Perugia, Italy; d. Innsbruck, Austria 1841. Also a composer. Kapellmeister at Dresden (1810–19) where, despite his devious, vain behaviour, he proved a brilliant conductor and trainer.

MORRIS, Wyn, b. 1929. Founder-Conductor, Welsh Symphony Orchestra (1954–57). Later posts have included a number of choral ones, including Royal Choral Society (1968–70) and Huddersfield Choral Society (1969–74). Conductor, Symphonica of London.

MOTTL, Felix, b. 1856, Unter-Sankt-Veit, Germany; d. Munich, 1911. Also a composer. He assisted Wagner at the first *Ring* (1876) at Bayreuth, where he later conducted regularly (1888–1902). Wagner considered his *Tristan* the finest he had heard. Very successful at Karlsruhe (1891–1904) not only for his Wagner and Mozart, but for his performance of the first complete *Les Troyens* of Berlioz. At Covent Garden (1898–1900) and Metropolitan, New York (1903–04), also Munich (1903–11), as Director from 1907. He collapsed during a *Tristan* in which his mistress, Zdenka Fassbender, was the Isolde and had just sung 'Death-doomed heart'. Despite the heart attack that hit him at that moment, he survived to marry his Isolde on his deathbed.

MRAVINSKI, Yevgeni, b. 1903, St. Petersburg, Russia. Opera and Ballet Theatre, Leningrad (1932–38). Leningrad State Philharmonic Orchestra (1938–). This major conductor has made concert tours to Britain, the USA and in many European countries.

MUCK, Karl, b. 1859, Darmstadt, Germany; d. Stuttgart, 1940. Beginning as a pianist, he became a conductor in 1884. After posts at Salzburg, Graz and Brno, he became Conductor at Prague's Landestheater (1886–92). Gave the first Russian *Ring* (1889) with Neumann's Wagner Company. Berlin State Opera (1892–1912), Generalmusikdirektor (from 1908). He conducted 1,071 performances of 103 operas there, 35 of them being new, a feat worthy of the Guinness Book of Records. He was at Bayreuth (1901–30), where his *Parsifal* was acclaimed as the finest of its period. With the Boston Symphony Orchestra (1912–17) until dismissed as an enemy alien and imprisoned, after allegedly refusing to conduct *The Star-Spangled Banner*. He returned to Europe after the war, becoming a guest conductor, then Conductor of the Hamburg Philharmonic (1922–33). Greatly admired, he shared with Toscanini a belief in the score, unlike many earlier conductors. He was impatient and sarcastic and no respecter of reputations but he was a deeply serious musician who conducted much music that was uncongenial to him from a sense of duty. Totally untheatrical on the podium, he excelled in Wagner, Mahler and Bruckner.

MUDIE, Michael, b. 1914, Manchester, England; d. Brussels, Belgium, 1962. Carl Rosa Opera (1935–39). Sadler's Wells Opera (1946–53). Ill-health caused his early retirement. Widely regarded as a highly promising operatic conductor, especially in Italian works.

MUGNONE, Leopoldo, b. 1858, Naples, Italy; d. Naples, 1941. Also a composer, who wrote an opera produced when he was twelve. Conducted a season of opera in Venice aged sixteen. Gave the premières of *Cavalleria Rusticana* (Rome, 1890) and *Tosca* (Rome, 1900). At La Scala (from 1880), and also conducted at Covent Garden (1905–06: 1919–24) and at the Metropolitan Opera, New York (1922). Regarded as an outstanding conductor of Italian opera, the best of his period according to Beecham.

MUNCH, Charles, b. 1891, Strasbourg, (then in) Germany; d. Richmond, Virginia, USA, 1968. Originally a violinist, becoming the leader of the Leipzig Gewandhaus Orchestra. Conducting debut (1932) with Straram Orchestra. He formed the Paris Philharmonic, becoming Musical Director of the Paris Conservatoire Orchestra (1937). With the previous orchestras he had given much contemporary music; now he lifted his new orchestra to its earlier heights. After the war, in which his earnings had helped the Resistance, he became an international figure: Edinburgh Festival, Prague, London (where he had first appeared in 1938) and the USA. He succeeded Koussevitsky with the Boston Symphony Orchestra (1949–62), taking it on a European tour, including Moscow and Leningrad, in 1956. At his considerable best, he was noted for his elegant, polished performances.

MÜNCHINGER, Karl, b. 1915, Stuttgart, Germany. Founder and Conductor, Stuttgart Chamber Orchestra (1945–).

MUNROW, David, b. 1942; d. St. Albans, Herts, 1976. British. An expert on early music and Founder/Director of the Early Music Consort of London (1967). He was an inspired broadcaster.

MUTI, Riccardo, b. 1941, Naples, Italy. Currently (1979–) Principal Conductor, Philharmonia Orchestra, this brilliant young conductor won the Guido Cantelli Conducting Competition (1967), then rapidly made his name in Italy, conducting concerts and opera. His operatic debut in Florence (I Puritani, 1971) was followed by other performances that showed he was a born operatic conductor. Salzburg debut with *Don Pasquale* 1971. His Covent Garden debut (*Aida*, 1977) had Alan Blyth writing of Muti's 'taut Toscanini-like direction'. Principal Guest Conductor, Philadelphia Orchestra (1976). Artistic Director, Florence Festival (1977–). His repertory is already vast. Apart from his superb Italian opera performances, he ranges from Stravinsky and Prokofiev through Tchaikovsky and Schumann, back to Beethoven and Cherubini. Musical Director, Philadelphia Orchestra (1980–).

NÁPRAVNIC, Eduard, b. 1839, Byst, Bohemia; d. St. Petersburg, Russia, 1916. Also a composer. After studying in Prague, he went to Russia (1861) to conduct Prince Yussopov's private orchestra. At the Maryinsky, St. Petersburg (1867), becoming Conductor (1869). He conducted more than 4,000 opera performances and reorganized Russia's opera houses, helped singers and musicians, and gave many world premières including Tchaikovsky's *Queen of Spades* (1890), and Mussorgsky's *Boris Godunov* (1874).

NAVARRO, Garcia, b. Chiva, Spain. Chief Conductor, Valencia Orchestra (1970–74). Lisbon Symphony Orchestra (1976–78). Associate Conductor, Northern Philharmonic Orchestra, Holland (1979–). Regular guest appearances in concerts and opera at home and abroad.

NEEL, Boyd, b. 1905, London, England. After a career as a doctor, he founded and conducted the Boyd Neel Orchestra (1932), except during World War Two, when he returned to medicine. Guest appearances included Salzburg (1937) and Sadler's Wells Opera (1945). Dean, Royal Conservatory of Music, Toronto (1953–71). Formed the Hart House Orchestra (1955–), performing in Canada and Europe.

NEUMANN, František, b. 1874, Prerov, Bohemia; d. Brno, Czechoslovakia, 1929. Also composer. Prague (1906–19). Brno (1919–29). He conducted the premières of three Janáček operas: *Sarka, Káťa Kabanová, The Cunning Little Vixen,* and *The Makropoulos Case.*

NEUMANN, Vaclav, b. 1920, Prague, Czechoslovakia. Made his debut in Prague, replacing Kubelik who was ill (1948). At Carlsbad and Brno, then Conductor, Prague Symphony Orchestra (1956–63) and Prague Philharmonic Orchestra (1963–64). Chief Conductor, Komische Oper Berlin (1957–60). Gewandhaus Orchestra of Leipzig and Generalmusikdirektor, Leipzig Opera (1964–67). Chief Conductor, Czech Philharmonic Orchestra (1968–). Music Director, Württembergische Staatsoper (1969–72). Many foreign tours.

NEWSTONE, Harry, b. 1921, Winnipeg, Canada. Founder/Conductor, Haydn Orchestra (1949–). Musical

Director, Conductor, Sacramento Symphony Orchestra, (1965–1978). Has conducted leading orchestras in Britain, Europe and North America.

NICOLAI, Otto, b. 1810, Königsberg, Germany; d. Berlin, 1849. The composer of *Die lustigen Weiber von Windsor*, he was also a distinguished conductor. Kapellmeister, then First Kapellmeister, Karntnertortheater (1841–47). Founder of the Vienna Philharmonic Orchestra (1842), conducting in until 1848. Director, Royal Opera, Berlin (1847–49). Berlioz greatly admired his conducting.

NIKISCH, Artur, b. 1855, Lebenyi, Szent-Miklos, Hungary; d. Leipzig,

Artur Nikisch could mesmerize his players. Other conductors, even Toscanini, admired him greatly.

Germany, 1922. Began as a violinist and pianist. One of the most admired of all conductors, notably by musicians, and he was also remarkable in that he was loved as a person and had no enemies. We are told that he could mesmerize his players. Sir Adrian Boult declared that he 'made his stick say more than any other conductor I have ever seen'. He could transform any orchestra he conducted. Even other great conductors admired him. An improvisatory conductor, one of his most famous disciples was Furtwängler.

He was Chorus Master at Leipzig (1877), becoming First Conductor there (1879–89). With the Boston Symphony Orchestra (1889–93). Director, Budapest Opera (1893–95). Leipzig Gewandhaus (1895–1922). Berlin Philharmonic Orchestra (1896–1922). He was also a guest conductor with many orchestras, including the London Symphony Orchestra. His beat was minimal, his achievement massive. Even Toscanini responded to him with warmth. Nikisch conducted at La Scala, then complimented Toscanini on the orchestra's high quality. 'I happen to know this orchestra very well,' said the maestro. 'I am conductor of this orchestra. It is a bad orchestra. You are a good conductor.'

NORRINGTON, Roger, b. 1934, Oxford, England. Musical Director, Kent Opera (1966–), which has gone from strength to strength under his direction. He has conducted the English National Opera, London Symphony Orchestra, Royal

Philharmonic Orchestra, the Schütz Choir and has appeared abroad. His realizations of Monteverdi have been widely acclaimed for their authenticity, being less lush than Raymond Leppard's. Fortunately it is not the business of this author to take sides.

OBERHOFFER, Emil, b. 1867, nr. Munich, Germany; d. San Diego, California, USA, 1933. Founder of the Minneapolis Symphony Orchestra (1903–22).

OFFENBACH, Jacques, b. 1819, Cologne, Germany; d. Paris, 1880. The great operetta composer was also a conductor and cellist.

ORMANDY, Eugene, b. 1899, Budapest, Hungary. After starting as an infant prodigy violinist (entering the Budapest Conservatory at five), he came to the USA (1921), becoming Conductor of the Minneapolis Symphony Orchestra (1931–36), then Music Director and Conductor of the Philadelphia Orchestra (1938–80), having shared two seasons with Stokowski. By common consent, the orchestra maintained its fame as one of the supreme virtuoso orchestras – some would say it is the finest of all. Despite this, Ormandy himself has been constantly denied the accolade of greatness. Accused of too much *portamento*, too rich a sound, too shallow an approach to music etc, the fact remains his lush readings of the late romantic repertoire are given with great authority, and he is renowned for his speed in mastering a score, his memory and his musical ear – and, with his orchestra, for the 'Philadelphia Sound'. In 1980, he retired, becoming Conductor Laureate, his place being taken by Riccardo Muti.

OZAWA, Seiji, b. 1935, Hoten, Japan. Studied with Karajan and Bernstein. Assistant Conductor, New York

Seiji Ozawa is a triumphant symbol of Japan's recent discovery of, and passion for, Western arts.

Philharmonic (1961–62). Musical Director, Ravinia Festival (1964–68). Principal Conductor, Toronto Symphony Orchestra (1965–69) and San Francisco Symphony Orchestra (1969–76). Director, Berkshire Festival, Tanglewood, Mass. (1970–), Musical Director, Boston Symphony Orchestra (1973–). A wide-ranging guest conductor with the London Symphony Orchestra etc. He is admired by his musicians, not least for his rocket-like rise to the top in an alien musical tradition. His Covent Garden debut in *Eugene Onegin* (1974) was a brilliant one; it was only his second appearance in an opera pit. He led the Boston Symphony on a tour of China in 1979, a highlight of the home season being a stunning performance of Schoenberg's *Gurrelieder*. One of the leading younger conductors of the day. Made his debut at La Scala, Milan with *Tosca* (1980).

PALSSON, Páll, b. 1928, Graz, Austria. Also a composer. Originally a trumpeter, he became Conductor, Graz Philharmonic Orchestra (1945–49). Conductor, Reykjavik City Band (1949–73). Conductor, Iceland State Symphony Orchestra (1960–   ).

PANIZZA, Ettore, b. 1875, Buenos Aires, Argentina; d. Buenos Aires, 1967. Of Italian descent, this Argentinian studied in Milan. At Covent Garden (1907–1924). Toscanini's assistant at La Scala, Milan (1916–17: 1921–29) and, after Toscanini's departure (1930–32: 1946–48). Teatro Colon, Buenos Aires (1921–67). His Milan premières included Puccini's *Trittico* and Mussorgsky's *Khovanschina*.

PARIS, Alain, b. 1947, Paris, France. Has conducted widely in France and elsewhere, notably on radio and TV.

PARROTT, Andrew, b. 1947, Walsall, England. Conductor, Schola Cantorum, Oxford (1968–71). Musica Reservata (1973–76). Taverner Choir (1973–   ). Conducts at the Proms etc.

PATANÉ, Giuseppe, b. 1932, Naples, Italy. He has conducted opera widely in Italy, Germany and Austria. American debut, San Francisco Opera (1967). Covent Garden debut (1974).

PAUR, Emil, b. 1855, Czernowitz, Bohemia; d. Mistek, Czechoslovakia, 1932. Boston Symphony (1893–98). New York Philharmonic (1898–1902). Berlin Schauspielhaus (1912–13).

PEDROTTI, Carlo, b. 1817, Verona, Italy; d. Verona, 1893. Also a composer, famous in his own day. Director, Teatro Regio, Turin (1868–82) a most important period in the city's musical life. A leading Italian Wagnerian, he conducted a famous *Lohengrin* (1876). He also gave French operas, as well as a number of Italian premières.

PILBERY, Joseph, b. 1931, London, England. The Founder/Conductor of the New Westminster Philharmonic Orchestra (1972), with whom he is currently (1980) giving a Mahler cycle in London. Has also conducted the Royal Philharmonic Orchestra, London Mozart Players etc, and in France, Vienna, Holland, Switzerland and elsewhere. The Founder of the Sir Arthur Sullivan Society.

PINNOCK, Trevor, b. 1946, Canterbury, England. Also harpsichordist. Director, The English Concert.

PITT, Percy, b. 1870, London, England; d. London 1932. From 1902 regularly at Covent Garden. Music Director, Grand Opera Syndicate (1907–24). With Beecham Opera Company (1915–18). Artistic Director, British National Opera Company (1920–24). Musical Director, BBC (1924–30). His many Covent Garden premières included Mozart's *Bastien und Bastienne* and Mussorgsky's *Khovanschchina*.

POHLENZ, Christian, b. 1790, Sallgast, Germany; d. Leipzig, 1843. Indifferent to bad conductor of the Gewandhaus Orchestra, Leipzig, replaced by Mendelssohn.

POHLIG, Karl, b. 1858, Teplitz, Germany; d. Brunswick, 1928. Conductor, Philadelphia Orchestra (1907–12).

POLACCO, Giorgio, b. 1875, Venice, Italy; d. New York, 1960. A leading opera conductor of his day, including the première of Leoncavallo's *Zazà* (Milan, 1900). Conducted seven seasons in Rio de Janeiro, where he gave the first local *Bohème*, *Tosca*, *Boris Godunov* etc. At the Metropolitan, New York (1912–17) and Chicago Opera (1918–30), conducting many now legendary performances of French opera starring Mary Garden. Having originally made his conducting debut in London, taking over from an ill Arditi (1893), he appeared at Covent Garden (1913–14: 1930). Poor health forced his early retirement.

POOLE, John, b. 1934, Birmingham, England. Director, BBC Singers (1972–).

PRAUSNITZ, Frederick, b. 1920, Cologne, Germany. Debut, Detroit (1944). Has guest conducted widely in Britain and on the Continent (1957–), but is mainly based in the USA.

PRÊTRE, Georges, b. 1924, Waziers, France. This leading French conductor was Director of Music at Marseilles, Lille, Toulouse (1946–55). Musical Director, Opéra-Comique, Paris (1955–59). With the Paris Opéra (1959–), as Director General (1970–71). In the 1960s, he became internationally known, conducting the Berlin and Vienna Philharmonics, the Philharmonia, Royal Philharmonic, the Philadelphia etc. At La Scala, Milan (1965–), the Metropolitan, New York (1964–67), Covent Garden (1965: 1976), also the Chicago, San Francisco and Rome Operas and leading festivals.

PREVIN, André, b. 1930, Berlin, Germany. Also composer and pianist. Brought up in Los Angeles, and becoming American (1943), he wrote many film scores and arranged others, before turning to conducting. Music Director, Houston Symphony Orchestra (1967–69). Principal Conductor, London Symphony Orchestra (1968–1979), becoming Conductor Emeritus of the orchestra. Musical Director of the Pittsburg

Symphony Orchestra (1976–). A notable popularizer of music, not least because of his very easy manner as a speaker on TV, he has a remarkable sympathy for English music, including Vaughan Williams, all of whose symphonies he has recorded with the L.S.O., also with Walton. Like Bernstein, he has survived the suspicion of those who instinctively mistrust all-round talents.

PREVITALI, Fernando, b. 1907, Adria, Italy. Helped Vittorio Gui organize the Florence Orchestra and Festival (1928–35). Teatro Carlo Felice, Genoa (1935–36). The very influential Director of Radio Italiana Orchestra (1936–53). At La Scala, Milan (1942: 1947–48), also appearing in Rome, Buenos Aires and Naples. His many premières have included Dallapiccola's *Volo di Notte* (Florence, 1940). Conductor, Teatro San Carlo, Naples.

PRIESTMAN, Brian, b. 1927, Birmingham, England. Musical Director, Royal Shakespeare (1960–63). Edmonton Symphony Orchestra (1964–68). Denver Symphony Orchestra (1970–80). Principal Conductor, New Zealand Broadcasting Co. (1973–).

PRITCHARD, John, b. 1921, London, England. A very fine and experienced conductor of opera and concerts, his posts have included Conductor and Music Director, Royal Liverpool Philharmonic Orchestra (1957–63). Principal Conductor, London Philharmonic Orchestra (1962–66) and Music Director of Glyndebourne Festival Opera (1969–77), where he first conducted in 1952. At Covent Garden (1952–), the Metropolitan, New York (1971–), San Francisco Opera (1970–), Vienna State Opera (1952–53: 1964–65) also at Salzburg (1966) etc, and leading orchestras throughout the world. Chief Conductor Cologne Opera (1978–). His premières include Britten's *Gloriana*, and Tippett's *Midsummer Marriage* and *King Priam*, and his range is notably wide, including the 19th century Italian, German, French, Russian and Italian repertories. However, he is perhaps at his peak in Mozart.

QUADRI, Aregeo, b. 1911, Como, Italy. Directed the performance of *Traviata* at Busseto in 1950 to commemorate the 50th anniversary of the composer's death. Apart from appearing in the leading Italian opera houses, he was at the Volksoper, Vienna (1957–75).

RAABE, Peter, b. 1872, Frankfurt, Germany; d. Weimar, 1945. After conducting in Germany and Holland, became Court Conductor, Weimar (1907–20). Generalmusikdirektor, Municipal Orchestra, Aachen (1920–35) President of German Reichsmusikkammer (1935), succeeding Richard Strauss.

RABAGLINO, Emilio, b. 1942, Argentina. This Italo-Argentinian studied in Buenos Aires and Italy. La Plata Opera Theatre (1965–69). Permanent Conductor, Cordoba Symphony Orchestra (1969), also conducting all the leading Argentinian orchestras. Winner of International competitions in Florence (1976) and Budapest (1977), and has also conducted in Spain, Switzerland and Italy. A leading expert on de Falla.

RABAUD, Henri, b. 1873, Paris, France; d. Paris, 1949. Also a composer. Paris Opéra (1908–18), Director from 1914, Director Paris Conservatoire, (1920–40).

RAILTON, (Dame) Ruth, b. 1915, Folkestone, England. Also a pianist. Founder and Musical Director, National Youth Orchestra and National Junior Musical School (1947–65).

RANDEGGER, Alberto, b. 1832, Trieste, Italy; d. London, 1911. Also a composer. After posts in Italy, conducted the Carl Rosa (1879–85). Covent Garden and Drury Lane (1887–98). Conductor of The Norwich Festival, 1881–1905. Became a British citizen.

RANKL, Karl, b. 1898, Gaaden, Austria; d. St. Gilgen, 1968. Also a composer. His early posts included Kroll Opera, Berlin (1928–31) as Klemperer's assistant; Weisbaden (1931–32); Graz (1932–37) and Prague (1937–39), coming to Britain in 1939. After a spell of internment, he conducted leading British orchestras, becoming the first Music Director of the new Covent Garden Opera Co. (now the Royal Opera) in 1946. His reign was stormy because of the difficulties of forming a company from nothing and equally because his personality grated. And as a conductor he was not of the first rank, though his Strauss was admired. Yet when he resigned the foundations had been laid. Music Director, Elizabethan Opera Trust, Australia (1958–60).

RATTLE, Simon, b. 1955, Liverpool, England. One of the most gifted young conductors of the day, he won the 1974 International Conductors Competition, and became Assistant Conductor, Bournemouth Symphony Orchestra. He made his debut with the English Chamber Orchestra, Northern Sinfonia and the Royal Liverpool Philharmonic Orchestra, then, in 1976, his professional Royal Festival Hall debut with the Philharmonia, the youngest conductor ever to appear with the orchestra. With them, he conducted the world Première of Peter Maxwell Davies's First Symphony (1978). He has conducted in Europe and America, including the Los Angeles Philharmonic (1979), and will be returning annually. He first worked in opera on the music staff of Glyndebourne in 1975, later conducting *The Rake's Progress* for the Touring Company. He became the youngest ever Glyndebourne Festival conductor in 1977, with *The Cunning Little Vixen*. He will be continuing with the company into the '80s. At the Proms (1976–). He has been appointed Principal Conductor and

Simon Rattle, born as recently as 1955, has risen to fame at phenomenal and much acclaimed speed.

Artistic Adviser, City of Birmingham Orchestra (1980–82).

REICHARDT, Johann, b. 1752, Königsberg, Germany; d. Giebichenstein, 1814. Frederick the Great's Kapellmeister (1776–94), he was a pioneer who directed singers and orchestra from a desk near the footlights placed in the centre of the orchestra. He may have used a baton and certainly wanted the control his successors expected by right. Also a violinist and pianist.

REID, Ian, b. 1942, Scotland. After posts at Oldenburg and in Schleswig-Holstein (1965–67), he became First Conductor and Head of Music Staff, Stadttheater, Heidelberg (1970–73). Assistant Music Director, Hagen Opera (1973) becoming a Staff Conductor with the English National Opera (1976). He has also conducted at the Dubrovnik and other festivals, and the BBC Scottish Symphony Orchestra etc.

REIMUELLER, Ross, b. 1937, Dayton, Ohio, USA. Since his debut at Denver, Colorado with Puccini's *La Rondine* (1963), he has conducted opera at San Francisco and the New York City Opera, also the Metropolitan Opera National Co. (1965–67), also light opera and musicals.

REINECKE, Carl, b. 1824, Altona, Germany; d. Leipzig, Germany, 1910. At Leipzig (1860–95) in charge of the Gewandhaus Orchestra. An efficient conductor whose reputation suffered when the genius Nikisch took over the orchestra.

REINER, Fritz, b. 1888, Budapest, Hungary; d. New York, 1963. This perfectionist and supreme baton technician made his conducting debut as Chorus Master in *Carmen* in Budapest (1909). After other engagements, he was First Conductor, Dresden (1914–21), then went to the USA. Famous for his big baton and little beat, he was a great teacher (at the Curtis Institute, 1931–41), one pupil being Bernstein. His posts included the Chicago Symphony (1955–62) and the Metropolitan Opera, New York (1949–53). He conducted the Philadelphia in *Tristan*, *Falstaff* and *Rosenkavalier* and was in the pit at Covent Garden for Flagstad's legendary London debut as Isolde (1932). At San Francisco Opera (1936–38). Almost as tough with his players as Toscanini, whom he resembled in many ways, he was greatly respected, if not loved, by his players, not least because of his determination to get to the heart of a score by brushing aside romanticism and tradition.

REISSIGER, Karl, b. 1798, Belzig, Germany; d. Dresden, Germany, 1859. Also a composer. At Dresden (1826–59), where his amiable, easy-going reign upset a young fellow-conductor, Richard Wagner, in 1843. However, he prepared the première of *Rienzi* (1842) and championed Wagner along with Beethoven and Weber.

RENNERT, Wolfgang, b. 1922, Cologne. A very experienced conductor since the late '40s, his posts have included Musical Director at Kiel (1950–53) and Frankfurt (1956–67). A regular conductor with the Berlin State Opera and other leading German houses, he is particularly known for his Richard Strauss. Has conducted many European orchestras, and at Salzburg, a much admired debut at Covent Garden in *Arabella* (1977).

RICHTER, Hans, b. 1843, Gyor, Hungary; d. Bayreuth, Germany, 1916. Originally a horn player, he worked with Wagner at Triebschen as copyist etc. (1866–67). The young man who could play every orchestral instrument was recommended by Wagner to Bülow at Munich. He made his debut there with *Guillaume Tell* (1868) and even sang in *Meistersinger* as Kothner. Resigned (1869) as he disliked a production of *Rheingold* which was being prepared, as, presumably, did Wagner. Gave the first Belgian *Lohengrin* (1870). At the National Opera, Budapest (1871–75). In Vienna (opera and concerts, 1875–1900), as Musical Director (1893–1900). Began the Richter concerts in England (1879–1911), where he was in charge of the Hallé Orchestra (1897–1911), giving the première of Elgar's First Symphony.

Richter was at Bayreuth (1876–1912), where he conducted the first *Ring* (1876). At Drury Lane, London, he conducted the first English *Tristan* and *Meistersinger* and at Covent Garden (1903–10) he gave his historic *Ring* in English. Through no fault of his own he failed to found an English National Opera. He gave the world premières of Bruckner's Fourth Symphony (1891), also Brahms' Second (1877) and Third (1883).

Faced with this massive achievement, it is odd to discover that Richter was not the most imaginative of conductors and that his interpretations were on the deliberate side, according to some. Bülow and Wagner himself were not totally satisfied with him. His repertory was small, yet audiences and orchestral musicians responded to his qualities as a man and a conductor, and Debussy considered him the supreme Wagnerian. Mozart, however, was ponderous under him. The contradictions in reports of him are puzzling, yet he was an undeniable giant. Perhaps *Meistersinger* was his most acclaimed interpretation.

RICKENBACHER, Karl, b. 1940, Basle, Switzerland. A leading Swiss conductor. Guest appearances in Germany, Italy etc. Principal Conductor, BBC Scottish Symphony Orchestra (1977).

ROBERTSON, James, b. 1912, Liverpool, England. His career has been almost entirely in opera, most notably as Director and Conductor of Sadler's Wells Opera (1946–54) and as Director of the Opera Centre (1964–78). He has also conducted in New Zealand, including as Artistic Director, New Zealand Opera and Conductor, Concert Orchestra of the New Zealand Broadcasting Co. (1962–63).

ROBINSON, Stanford, b. 1904, Leeds, England. With BBC (1924–66), conducting its orchestras and choirs. Conducted at Covent Garden and Sadler's Wells, then he conducted in

Australia and New Zealand. His brother was the popular TV conductor, Eric Robinson.

RODAN, Mendi, b. 1929, Jassy, Romania. Permanent Conductor, Radio-TV Orchestra, Bucharest (1953–58). Chief Conductor and Musical Director, Jerusalem Symphony Orchestra (1963–72). Permanent Guest Conductor, Israeli Philharmonic Orchestra. He has conducted in Europe, the Americas, South Africa and Australia.

RODZINSKI, Artur, b. 1892, Split, Dalmatia; d. Boston, USA, 1958. A Pole, later naturalized American, he was at Warsaw Opera (1920–24). Emigrating, he joined the Curtis Institute, Philadelphia, and became a guest conductor in the USA. Los Angeles Philharmonic (1929–33). Cleveland Orchestra (1933–43). New York Philharmonic (1943–47). Chicago Symphony (1947–48), also guest appearances. A controversial figure, he sacked fourteen of the New York Philharmonic, including the concertmaster (leader) when taking over the orchestra, and he only lasted a season in Chicago. Yet his reputation as an orchestra builder was considerable, as was his ability with modern music. His American premières included Shostakovitch's *Lady Macbeth of the Mtsensk District* (1935). One of his many appearances in Italy was the first Western performance of Prokofiev's *War and Peace* (Florence, 1953).

RONALD, Landon, b. 1873, London, England; d. London, 1938. Also a composer and accompanist (of Melba etc). After some early operatic experience, he made his reputation conducting the orchestra of the Royal Philharmonic Society in place of Richter (1909). Conductor, Royal Albert Hall Orchestra (1909–19), Scottish Orchestra etc, but his career was shortened by ill-health. Knighted in 1922.

ROSBAUD, Hans, b. 1895, Graz, Austria; d. Lugano, Switzerland, 1962. Best remembered as a champion of Schoenberg, whose *Erwartung* and *Von Heute auf Morgen* he gave at the Holland Festival (1958). In charge of the première of *Moses und Aron* on radio (1954) and on stage (1957). His pre-war posts included Frankfurt, Mainz, Munster and Strasbourg, while he was Chief Conductor of the excellent Aix-en-Provence Festival (1947–59) from its inception.

ROSENSTOCK, Joseph, b. 1895, Cracow, Poland. Posts include Stuttgart (1921–22), Darmstadt (1925–27 and Wiesbaden (1927–28). Took over at the Metropolitan, New York, from Bodansky (1929), but resigned after a very short reign. At Mannheim (1930–33), then Musical Director, Jewish Kulturbund, Berlin (1933–36) until being forced to emigrate. Conductor, Symphony Orchestra of Tokyo (1936–41: 1945–46). Conductor and General Director, New York City Opera (1948–56). Cologne (1958–59). Metropolitan Opera during the 1960s.

ROSENTHAL, Manuel, b. 1904, Paris, France. Also a composer. Musical

Director and Conductor, National Orchestra of Paris (1945–48). Seattle Symphony Orchestra (1949–51). Royal Orchestra of Liège (1964–67). Professor of Orchestral Conducting, National Conservatoire of Paris (1962–   ).

ROSTROPOVICH, Mstislav, b. 1927, Baku, USSR. One of the world's greatest cellists, he has turned more and more to conducting concerts and opera. Director, National Symphony Orchestra, Washington (1977–   ). Married to the soprano, Galina Vishnevskaya, whose performances he first conducted in 1969. Regularly conducts the London Philharmonic Orchestra, including a Festival Hall cycle of the seven Tchaikovsky symphonies (1976). Artistic Director, Aldeburgh Festival. *Eugene Onegin*, Florence Festival (1980).

ROZHDESTVENSKY,   Gennadi, b. 1931, Moscow, USSR. Assistant Conductor,   Bolshoi,   Moscow (1951–56),   Conductor   (1956–60), Principal Conductor (1964–70). Chief Conductor, USSR Radio and TV Symphony Orchestra (1961–   ). Music Director, Stockholm Philharmonic Orchestra   (1975–78).   He   first conducted in London in 1956 with the Bolshoi Ballet, since when he has made many guest appearances in Europe and America. Currently

(1979–   ) Chief Conductor BBC Symphony Orchestra. Conducted *Boris* with the Bolshoi Opera in Paris, also with the Royal Opera, Covent Garden (1970).

ROZMARYNOWICZ, Andrzej, b. 1928, Poznanland, Poland. Debut, Katowice (1961). Guest conductor (1961–67), since when his posts have included   Director   and   Artistic Director,   Opera   House,   Cracow (1970–72) and Conductor, Wrocla Opera (1972–76).

RUBENSTEIN, Bernard, b. 1937, USA. A wide-ranging guest conductor of concerts and opera in America and Europe, he is Conductor and Director of Opera at Northwestern University, Chicago, where he gave the US première of Tippett's *The Knot Garden* (1974).

RUDEL, Julius, b. 1921, Vienna, Austria. Musical and Artistic Director, New York City Opera (1957–79), with a record   of   very   impressive achievements, including seasons of modern American opera. Music Director,   Kennedy   Center, Washington   (1971–76).   He   has conducted   at   the   Paris   Opéra (1972–   ), also at Stuttgart, Hamburg etc. A major figure in opera in the USA.   Musical   Director,   Buffalo Philharmonic Orchestra.

S

SAARI, Jouko, b. 1944, Stockholm, Sweden. Various posts in Sweden and elsewhere. Conductor, Tampere City Orchestra (1973–74). Conductor-Coach, Cologne Opera (1975–76) etc.

SABATA (see DE SABATA).

SACHER, Paul, b. 1906, Basle, Switzerland. Founder, Basle Chamber Orchestra (1926). Founder, Schola Cantorum Basiliensis 1933. Conductor, Collegium Musicum, Zurich (1941–). Director, Music Academy, Basle (1954–69). Has conducted in most European countries, including at leading festivals: Glyndebourne, Aix-en-Provence, Edinburgh etc.

SAFONOFF, Vassily, b. 1852, Ishtcherskaya, Russia; d. Kislovodsk, 1918. Also a pianist, a very noted one. Conducted in Moscow, then Conductor New York Philharmonic (1906–09). After a dynamic start, he seems only to have made his mark in Tchaikovsky.

SALMHOFFER, Franz, b. 1900, Vienna, Austria; d. Vienna, 1975. Also a composer. Conductor, Vienna Burgtheater (1929–39). Director, Volksoper (1955–75), having conducted at the State Opera from 1945. A descendant of Schubert.

SALZEDO, Leonard, b. 1921, London, England. Also a composer. Beginning as a violinist, he was Musical Director, Ballet Rambert (1966–72) and Principal Conductor, Scottish Theatre Ballet (1972–74).

SANDERLING, Kurt. b. 1915, Arys, East Germany. Assistant Conductor, Berlin Städtische Oper; leaving to conduct Moscow Radio Orchestra. There followed his noted period with the Leningrad Philharmonic Orchestra (1941–60), as co-Director with Mravinsky. Chief Conductor, Berlin. Staatsoper (1960–77). Director, Dresdner Staatskapelle Orchestra (1964–67). He has regularly conducted in Britain, first appearing in London with the Philharmonia, replacing Klemperer to whom he has often been compared. Also at Salzburg, Vienna etc. American debut in 1977. His son Thomas is also a conductor who has conducted widely abroad. His posts in East Germany include Senior Director of Music and Opera in Hallé (1966), becoming responsible for the Handel Festival there.

SANTI, Nello, b. 1931, Adria, Italy. Debut, Padua (1951), since when he has conducted opera in Italy and elsewhere, including Covent Garden, the Metropolitan, New York (1962–65) and in Germany. Also Zurich (1965–).

SANTINI, Gabriele, b. 1886, Perugia, Italy; d. Rome, 1964. Assistant to Toscanini at La Scala (1925–29). Rome Opera (1929–32: 1945–62), finally as Musical Director. He also conducted at Covent Garden, Chicago and Buenos Aires.

SANZOGNO, Nino, b. 1911, Venice, Italy. Also a composer. At La Scala, Milan (1941–), as a principal conductor since 1962. A brilliant conductor of modern works, including *Oedipus Rex*, *The Fiery Angel* and *Dialogues des Carmelites*, also a noted conductor of 18th century Italian opera. Conducted the opening performance of La Piccola Scala (1955).

SARGENT, (Sir) Malcolm, b. 1895, Stamford, England; d. London, 1967. One of the most popular of all British conductors, with audiences, especially Promenaders, and choral societies, though not with orchestral players, his contribution to the spreading of a love of music in Britain was immense. Originally an organist. Conductor, Courtauld-Sargent Concerts in London (1929–40) and the Robert Mayer Children's Concerts – he was very good with young audiences – also the Royal Choral Society (from 1928). Hallé Orchestra (1939). Liverpool Philharmonic Orchestra (1942). BBC Symphony Orchestra (1950–57),

remaining as Chief Conductor of the Proms until his death. A noted Gilbert and Sullivan enthusiast, he conducted the D'Oyly Carte Co. (1926–28). His premières included Vaughan Williams' *Hugh the Drover* (1924) and Walton's *Troilus and Cressida* (1954). Sargent could not get on with his players. 'He actually made you play worse,' says John Ronayne in *Orchestra*. Tactless remarks in 1936 about the inadvisability of giving players pensions hardly helped. See Charles Reid's *Malcolm Sargent*. Knighted in 1947.

SAWALLISCH, Wolfgang, b. 1923, Munich, Germany. Debut, Augsburg (1947), becoming Kapellmeister. Generalmusikdirektor, Aachen (1953–57), then at Wiesbaden (1957–59) and Cologne (1959–63). Bayreuth (1957–62). Generalmusikdirektor, Bavarian State Opera (1974–). Hamburg Philharmonic Orchestra (1960) Principal Conductor, Vienna Symphony Orchestra (1960). He has also conducted widely abroad.

SCHALK, Franz, b. 1863, Vienna, Austria; d. Edlach, Germany, 1931. After studying with Bruckner, he held various posts including Graz (1889–95), Prague (1895–98), Berlin (1899–1900), then Vienna (1900–31), as Director of the State Opera from 1918, and co-First Conductor with Richard Strauss. They fell out and Schalk remained in sole charge. He helped found the Salzburg Festival. At Covent Garden (1898: 1907: 1911) and Metropolitan, New York (1898–99). Conducted the première of Strauss's *Die Frau ohne Schatten* (Vienna, 1919). As well as being a fine Straussian, he was noted for his Wagner and Beethoven.

SCHEEL, Fritz, b. 1852, Lubeck, Germany; d. Philadelphia, USA, 1907. After conducting some fine concerts in Philadelphia, this friend of Brahms and Tchaikovsky inspired the founding of the Philadelphia Orchestra (1900), which he conducted until his death. His standards were very high.

SCHERCHEN, Hermann, b. 1891, Berlin, Germany; d. Florence, Italy, 1966. Originally a viola player with the Berlin Philharmonic, he conducted from 1911. Best known for his performances of modern music in the concert hall and opera house, also as author of *Handbook of Conducting*. His premières included Dalapicolla's *Il priginiero* (Florence, 1950) and Henze's *Konig Hirsh* (Berlin, 1956).

SCHERMAN, Thomas, b. 1917, New York, USA. Founder of the New York Little Orchestra Society (1947) especially noted for the number of less well-known operas it has performed in concert form.

SCHILLINGS, Max von, b. 1868, Duren, Germany; d. Berlin, 1933. Also a composer and manager. After working at Bayreuth, he was at Stuttgart (1908–18), becoming Generalmusikdirektor (1911). Intendant, Berlin (1919–25).

SCHIPPERS, Thomas, b. 1930, Kalamazoo, Michigan, USA; d. New York, 1977. His early death robbed America of a conductor of

international standing especially in opera. With Gian Carlo Menotti, he founded the Spoleto Festival (1958), having conducted the première of *The Consul* (New York, 1950). He also conducted other Menotti premières in America and Spoleto. Conducted the Premiére of Barber's *Antony and Cleopatra* (1966), which opened the new Metropolitan Opera; also conducted the New York Philharmonic and the New York City Opera. He made many guest appearances abroad, including *Meistersinger* at Bayreuth (1963) and *Elektra* at Covent Garden (1968). Conductor of the Cincinnati Symphony Orchestra (1970–77).

SCHMID, Erich, b. 1907, Balsthal, Switzerland. A leading conductor in Switzerland. Principal Guest Conductor, City of Birmingham Symphony Orchestra (1979–81).

SCHMIDT, Ole, b. 1928, Copenhagen, Denmark. Also a composer. With Royal Opera, Copenhagen (1958–65), then became a guest conductor. Chief Conductor, Hamburger Sinfoniker (1971–73). Appointed Conductor of Danish Radio Symphony Orchestra (1975). Has conducted widely in Europe and Britain.

SCHMIDT-ISSERSTEDT, Hans, b. 1900, Berlin, Germany; d. Hamburg, 1973. After conducting at Wuppertal, Rostock and Darmstadt, he became First Conductor, Hamburg State Opera (1935–43). Conductor in Chief, Radio Hamburg (1945) when he founded the Nordwestdeutcher Rundfunk Symphony Orchestra. He conducted *Tristan* at Covent Garden (1962).

SCHNEIDER, Friedrich, b. 1786, Alt-Waltersdorf, Germany; d. Dessau, Germany, 1853. Also a composer. Kapellmeister of the Duke of Anhalt-Desau (1821–53).

SCHUCH, Ernst von, b. 1846, Graz, Austria; d. Dresden, Germany, 1914. Debut Breslau (1867). Posts included Würzburg, Graz and Basle, then Dresden (1872–1914): Court Conductor (1873) and Generalmusikdirektor, Dresden Opera (1882–1914). A famous Wagnerian, he also introduced Puccini to Dresden and gave the premières of Strauss's *Der Feuersnot, Salome, Elektra* and *Rosenkavalier*. Strauss himself merely called him 'conscientious', but Schuch made Dresden one of the greatest opera houses of the day.

SCHÜLER, Johannes, b. 1894, Vietz, Germany; d. Berlin, 1966. After various posts he was at the Berlin Staatsoper (1936–49). Generalmusikdirektor, Hanover (1949–60), which he made famous for its wide repertory.

SCHULLER, Gunther, b. 1925, New York City, USA. Originally a horn player, and principally a composer, he has conducted most leading American orchestras and many European ones. Director of Music, New England Conservatory of Music, Boston.

SCHWARTZ, Rudolf, b. 1905, Vienna, Austria. After building a career between the wars, he was imprisoned in Belsen as a Jew. Musical Director, Bournemouth Symphony Orchestra (1947). City of Birmingham Symphony Orchestra (1951). BBC Symphony Orchestra (1957–62). Northern Sinfonia (1964).

SEAMAN, Christopher, b. 1942, Nr. Canterbury, England. Originally a percussionist. Principal Conductor, BBC Scottish Symphony Orchestra (1971–76) and the Northern Sinfonia, he is now (1980) Conductor and Artistic Adviser, the Gelders Orchestra, and Principal Guest Conductor, Utrecht Symphony Orchestra (both in Holland). Particularly good with young people he regularly conducts the National Youth Orchestra and is the Principal Conductor (1979–) of the BBC/Robert Mayer Children's Concerts.

SEBASTIAN, George, b. 1903, Budapest, Hungary. After working with Bruno Walter in Munich, he went to Leipzig (1924–27). Chief Conductor, Paris Opéra (1947–73). Many guest appearances in France and Switzerland.

SEGAL, Uri, b. 1944, Jerusalem, Israel. After studying in London, he won First Prize at the Mitropoulos International Conducting Competition in New York (1969) and became Assistant Conductor, New York Philharmonic (1969–70). Since then he has conducted all the leading British orchestras and toured Europe. New Zealand, Japan and America. Principal Conductor, Bournemouth Symphony Orchestra (1980–).

SEGERSTAM, Leif, b. 1944, Vasa, Finland. Also a composer and violinist. Finnish National Opera (1965–68). Royal Opera Stockholm (1968), becoming Principal Conductor (1971). Has been a guest conductor all over Europe. Currently, Conductor, Radio Symphony Orchestra, Helsinki.

SEIDL, Anton, b. 1850, Pest, Hungary; d. New York, 1898. Introduced to Wagner by Richter, he helped prepare the score of the *Ring* and was recommended by the composer to Neumann, Director of the Leipzig Opera, for the post of First Conductor (1879–82). Conducted Neumann's Wagner company on its European tour (1883), then went to Bremen (1883–85). At the Metropolitan, New York (1885–89), he gave the first American *Tristan, Meistersinger, Rheingold, Siegfried* and *Götterdämmerung*. Conducted London's first *Ring* (1882) at Her Majesty's. At Covent Garden (1897) and Bayreuth (1897), dying in his prime.

SEMKOW, Jerzy, b. 1928, Radomsko, Poland. Assistant Conductor, Leningrad Philharmonic Orchestra (1954–56), after which he became Conductor, Bolshoi, Moscow (1956–58) and Artistic Director and Principal Conductor, Warsaw National Opera (1959–61). He has conducted in London, Chicago, Switzerland, Italy etc. Became Permanent Conductor, Royal Opera, Copenhagen (1966). Gave a superb *Boris* – the original version – in Rome (1978).

SERAFIN, Tullio, b. 1878, Rottanova di Cavatzere, Italy; d. Rome, 1968.

Callas, Gobbi, Sutherland and many more singers owed and owe much to Tullio Serafin's teaching.

One of the great operatic conductors of the century, and a key figure in the early years of the careers of great singers, including Rosa Ponselle, Maria Callas, Tito Gobbi and Joan Sutherland. Debut, Ferrara (1900). At La Scala, Milan (1902: 1910–14; 1918: 1939–40: 1946–7). Covent Garden (1907: 1931: 1959–60). Metropolitan, New York (1924–34). Rome (1934–43), as Chief Conductor and Artistic Director, returning in 1962. Chicago Opera (1956–58). Though best known and highly acclaimed for his performances of Italian opera, he

ranged widely, his premières at the Metropolitan, including Gruenberg's *The Emperor Jones*, Deems Taylor's *Peter Ibbetson* and the American premières of *Turandot* and *La vida breve*. He gave the first Italian *Peter Grimes* at La Scala, and also had *Wozzeck* in his repertoire. His recordings with Callas in the 1950s are already legendary, as is the first Sutherland *Lucia* (Covent Garden, 1959), for which he coached her. His influence was colossal. See *My Life* by Tito Gobbi.

SEREBRIER, José, b. 1938, Monte Video, Uruguay. Also a composer. As well as conducting many leading American orchestras, this student of Copland at Tanglewood has conducted extensively in Europe and Israel. While Composer-in-Residence with the Cleveland Orchestra (1968–70), he was Music Director and Conductor of the Cleveland Philharmonic. He was also Associate Conductor of the American Symphony Orchestra for four years.

SHERMAN, Alec, b. 1907, London, England. Originally a violinist. A conductor from 1938, he founded the New London Orchestra (1941). Sadler's Wells Ballet (1943–45) and many guest appearances in Britain and elsewhere.

SILIPIGNI, Alfredo, b. 1931, Atlantic City, New Jersey, USA. Artistic Director and Conductor, New Jersey Opera Theatre (1965–). Has conducted widely elsewhere in US and overseas, mainly in opera.

SILLEM, Maurits, b. Switzerland. Associate Conductor, Glyndebourne (1951–56), also touring with Carl Rosa Opera and conducting over 400 performances. Joined Music Staff, Covent Garden (1960), becoming Head (1973–75). Has conducted opera for the English National Opera, Australian Opera, and at Covent Garden, including *Salome*, *Bohème*, *Jenufa* and *Parsifal*.

SILOTI, Alexander, b. 1863, nr. Charkov, Russia; d. New York, 1945. Best known as a pianist, he became Conductor of the Moscow Philharmonic (1901–02), after which he conducted widely in Russia, especially in St. Petersburg. Escaped (1919), finally settling in the USA.

SIMON, Emil, b. 1936, Chisinau, Romania. Permanent Conductor, Cluj State Philharmonic Orchestra (1960), since when he has conducted widely, especially in Eastern Europe.

SIMONOV, Yuri, b. 1941, Saratov, USSR. Kislovodosk Philharmonic Society (1967–69). Bolshoi, Moscow (1969–). becoming Chief Conductor (1970). He has toured Western Europe with the Bolshoi Opera.

SLATKIN, Leonard, b. 1944, Los Angeles. Originally a pianist, this American conductor is Musical Director, St. Louis Symphony Orchestra (1979–), having previously been Musical Director and Principal Conductor, New Orleans Philharmonic Orchestra (1977–79), which he still conducts. Has conducted most leading British orchestras (1974–), also in Europe, including the USSR.

SMALLENS, Alexander, b. 1889, St. Petersburg, Russia; d. Tucson, USA, 1972. Boston Opera (1911–14). Chicago Opera (1919–22). Musical Director, Philadelphia Civic Opera (1924–31). He also worked in Paris, Madrid, and as conductor of the Robin Hood Dell, Philadelphia.

SMITH, Julian, b. 1944, Worcester Park, England. Welsh National Opera as Chorus Master and Conductor (1973), including the Company's *Madam Butterfly*, produced by Joachim Herz, which is virtually the original *Butterfly* of 1904 (later revised by

Puccini). Smith is producing a new critical edition for Ricordi.

SNELL, Howard, Conductor, the Wren Orchestra. Ex-trumpeter of London Symphony Orchestra.

SOKOLOFF, Nikolai, b. 1886, Kiev, Russia; d. La Jolla, California, 1965. First conductor of the Cleveland Orchestra (1918–33).

SOLTI, (Sir) Georg, b. 1912, Budapest, Hungary. Starting as a pianist, he began conducting at the Budapest Opera (1933–39). Assistant to

Hungarian-born Georg Solti raised Covent Garden to international status. The result was a knighthood.

Toscanini at Salzburg (1937). In Switzerland throughout the war (being Jewish), he became the Musical Director of the Bavarian State Opera (1947–52), then Musical Director at Frankfurt (1952–61). Meanwhile, he had first conducted the London Philharmonic Orchestra in 1947, conducting it many times until becoming Principal Guest Conductor (1971) and Principal Conductor and Artistic Director (1979–). While at Frankfurt, he was a guest conductor with various orchestras, and conducted at Salzburg during the '50s. His Covent Garden debut was in 1959 (*Rosenkavalier*), and he became Musical Director (1961–71). Though the groundwork had already been done, Solti was chiefly responsible for making Covent Garden a great international opera house, and he himself conducted a wide repertory. His *Ring* divided opinion, as nearly everyone's does, but its dramatic achievement was generally acclaimed. He proved a wonderful Straussian and a thrilling Verdian. He has returned fairly regularly to London. Having become a British citizen, he was knighted in 1971.

Since 1969, he has been the Musical Director of the Chicago Symphony, and was the Musical Director of the Paris Opéra (1972–75). With Rolf Libermann, he re-established the Opéra as a great house, and has conducted there since. In 1978, he returned to his homeland for the first time in forty years, conducting two concerts with the Vienna Philharmonic.

A restless, dynamic figure on and off the podium, he is much liked by some players, less liked by others. In the opera house, the tension he generates sometimes results in strained first nights, rectified in later performances. Yet the excitement he brings is tremendous.

SPETRINO, Francesco, b. 1857, Palermo, Sicily; d. Rome, 1948. A leading conductor in Italy (1876–93). Warsaw Opera (1894–97). Vienna (1904–08). Metropolitan, New York (1980–09). Gave up his career in World War One. Also a composer.

SPOHR, Louis, b. 1784, Brunswick, Germany; d. Kassel, Germany, 1859. This once famous composer played a crucial part in conducting history related in Chapter 1.

SPONTINI, Gasparo, b. 1774, Maiolati, Italy; d. Maiolati, 1851. Best remembered for his operas, especially *La Vestale*, he was one of the first modern conductors. Overbearing and aggressive, he demanded and got innumerable rehearsals and became known as the Napoleon of the Orchestra. Also see Chapters 1 and 3.

STAERN, Gunner, b. 1922, Stockholm, Sweden; Chief Conductor, Gavle Philharmonic Orchestra (1954–62). Wexford Festival Opera (1963–65). Chief Conductor, Göteborg Opera (1969). He has conducted all over Europe.

STAPLETON, Robin, b. 1946, Horley, England. Music Staff, Covent Garden (1968–). He made his Festival Hall debut with the Royal Philharmonic Orchestra (1973), the year he began conducting regularly at Covent Garden. He has also conducted Glyndebourne Touring Opera etc.

STEINBACH, Fritz, b. 1855, Grünsfeld, Germany; d. Munich, 1916. Also a composer. Conductor of the Meiningen Orchestra (1886–1902), visiting Britain and elsewhere. Also conducted London Symphony Orchestra. Admired by Brahms.

STEINBERG, William, b. 1899, Cologne, Germany; d. New York, 1978 Klemperer's assistant at Cologne (1920). Prague (1925–29), then Generalmusikdirektor at Frankfurt (1929–33) until sacked by the Nazis. Music Director of Jewish Culture League, Germany (1933–36). Associate Conductor, NBC Symphony Orchestra (1938–41). Other posts included London Philharmonic Orchestra (1958–60) and Boston Symphony Orchestra (1969). Principal Guest Conductor, New York Philharmonic (1964–68). He guest conducted all over the world. A noted interpreter of Wagner, Strauss and Verdi.

STEINITZ, Paul, b. 1909, Chichester, England. Conductor and Founder, London Bach Society and Steinitz Bach Players.

STERNBERG, Jonathan, b. 1919, New York City, USA. Debut with Vienna Symphony Orchestra (1947), after which he conducted widely in Europe and North and South America. Musical Director, Royal Flemish Opera (1961) and has conducted opera and ballet in the USA.

STERNEFELD, Daniel, b. 1905, Antwerp, Belgium. Also a composer. His long career has been mainly in Belgium orchestras, including the Symphony Orchestra of Belgian Broadcasting and the Royal Flemish Opera.

STEVENS, Denis, b. 1922, High Wycombe, England. This brilliant musicologist was conductor of the Ambrosian Singers (1956–60). An expert in pre-Classical music.

STIEDRY, Fritz, b. 1883, Vienna, Austria; d. Zurich, Switzerland, 1968. After conducting at Dresden etc, he became Kapellmeister at the Berlin Opera (1914–23). Succeeded Weingartner at the Vienna Volksoper (1924–28) also conducting concerts. At the Berlin Städtische Opera (1928–33), taking over from Bruno Walter as Chief Conductor (1929). With the producer Carl Ebert was a leader in the German Verdi renaissance. Their productions of *Macbeth* and *Simon Boccanegra* were renowned. Steidry gave the premières of Weill's *Die Bürgschaft* and Schoenberg's *Die glückliche Hand*. Because of the Nazis, he fled to Russia (1933–37), conducting the Philharmonic Society in Leningrad etc. Going to the USA, he was appointed Director of New Friends of Music Orchestra, New York (1938), later conducting the New Opera Co., New York, also at the Chicago Opera (1945–46) and the Metropolitan, New York (1946–58). He gave many notable Wagner and Verdi performances. In Britain, he conducted at Glyndebourne (1947) and Covent Garden (1953–54).

STOCK, Frederick, b. 1872, Julich, Germany; d. Chicago, USA, 1942. Also a composer and violist. This ex-army bandmaster was a violist in the Cologne Orchestra and the Chicago Symphony Orchestra, succeeding Theodore Thomas as Conductor of the latter (1905–43), a period of remarkable achievement.

STOKOWSKI, Leopold, b. 1882, London, England; d. Nether Wallop, England, 1977. Of Polish-Irish descent, he became one of the great figures in American musical history. He was naturalised in 1915. The great virtuoso conductor reached the USA as an organist, becoming Conductor of the

Leopold Stokowski's detractors could hardly argue with his Philadelphia Orchestra's excellence.

Cincinnati Symphony Orchestra (1909–12), where he proved his remarkable ability and drawing power. With the Philadelphia Orchestra (1912–36). His early programmes contained much modern music, including Schoenberg, Berg and Vaughan Williams. It was now that he began to introduce his Bach transcriptions. Always in the news, for his private life and appearances in films, most notably in Disney's *Fantasia,* also for his habit of changing his orchestra's seating positions, and for lecturing his audiences, his fame grew and grew. He would alter Beethoven and Brahms to make them 'grander', while his Bach adaptations enraged musicians even more. Yet this arrant showman was truly a master of the orchestra and of the possibilities of orchestral sound. The Philadelphia Orchestra's achievement under him was colossal, its virtuosity unsurpassed. He conducted them with his hands, having abandoned a baton early in his career. From 1936, he was a guest conductor with the Philadelphia. He founded the American Symphony Orchestra in 1962, he appeared with many leading American orchestras and at the Metropolitan (*Turandot*). And unlike many leading conductors, he remained interested in modern music. Despite his many professional detractors, he never lost his adoring public.

STRANSKY, Josef, b. 1872, Hupolec, Bohemia; d. New York, USA, 1936. Chief Conductor, Prague Landestheater (1898–1903) and at Hamburg Stadttheater (1903–11). He succeeded

Mahler with the New York Philharmonic (1911–21) with increasingly unhappy results.

STRAUSS, Richard, b. 1864, Munich, Germany; d. Garmisch-Partenkirchen, 1949. The great composer was also one of the great conductors of his day in the concert hall and in German opera, especially in Mozart. At Munich as third conductor of the Opera (1886–89), Weimar (1889–94) and Berlin (1898–1918), then co-Director with Franz Schalk of the Vienna Staatsoper (1919–24). He made frequent guest appearances with leading European and American orchestras. His beat was unobtrusively small and as his career progressed, he became more and more anti-romantic in his approach to music, including his own.

STROMBERGS, Alfred, b. 1922, Liepaja, Latvia. Since the 1950s, his career has been mainly in Canada. Founder and Conductor of the Halifax Symphony Orchestra (1951–55), since when he has played a leading role in Canadian operatic, theatrical and concert life.

SUMMERS, Michael, b. 1952, Stockholm, Sweden of British and German parents. Cape Town Symphony Orchestra (1979). Pomeriggi Musicale, Milan (1980). Founder, Orchestra Ambrosiana (1980). Operatic debut, Teatro Angelicum, Milan (1980) with Salieri's *Arlicchinata*.

SUSSKIND, Walter, b. 1913, Prague, Czechoslovakia; d. California 1980.

German Opera House, Prague (1933–38). Carl Rosa Opera (1943–45). As well as guest appearances with Sadler's Wells Opera and Glyndebourne (at the Edinburgh Festival), Principal Conductor, Scottish National Opera (1946–52). Principal Conductor, Victorian Symphony Orchestra, Melbourne (1953–55), after which he worked chiefly in Canada and the USA, including as Director, National Youth Orchestra of Canada and Director, Aspen Music Festival, Colorado (1961–68). From 1968, he made the St. Louis Symphony a major American orchestra. Guest appearances in many countries. Musical Adviser, Cincinnati Symphony Orchestra. His death caused many gaps in the 1980 British season.

SVETLANOV, Yevgeny, b. 1928, Moscow, USSR. Also a composer. Bolshoi Theatre (1954–62). Conductor, USSR State Symphony Orchestra (1965–). His many guest appearances include (1980) a series of concerts with the Philharmonia, also concerts with the London Symphony Orchestra.

SWOBODA, Henry, b. Prague, Czechoslovakia. Posts include Prague Opera, Dusseldorf Opera, Prague Broadcasting. A wide-ranging guest conductor, now based in the USA.

SZELL, Georg, b. 1897, Budapest, Hungary; d. Cleveland, USA, 1970. A child prodigy pianist, it was Richard Strauss who suggested he should become a conductor. His early posts included Strasbourg, Darmstadt and Dusseldorf. First Kapellmeister, Berlin

State Opera (1924–29), then Generalmusikdirektor, German Opera, Prague (1929–37). Went to the USA, becoming a US citizen, Metropolitan, New York (1942–46), where his Wagner and Strauss were much admired. He transformed the Cleveland Orchestra (1946–70) from a good to a great one, renowned for its ensemble. Not one to mince words, he made many enemies: To those who said he was his own worst enemy, Rudolf Bing retorted: 'Not while I'm alive.' Yet his many admirers hailed his performances of the German repertory from Haydn to Mahler.

SZENKÁR, Eugen, b. 1891, Budapest, Hungary; d. Dusseldorf, Germany, 1977. His many posts in Germany included Generalmusikdirektor, Cologne (1924–33) and Generalmusikdirektor, Dusseldorf (1952–56). He also conducted in Russia, Holland, Belgium, Spain, France and South America.

TABACHNIK, Michel, b. 1942, Geneva, Switzerland. Also a composer. Permanent Conductor, Gulbenkian Orchestra, Lisbon (1973–75). Regional Orchestra of Lorraine, France (1975–76). Artistic Director, Ensemble Inter-Contemporain, Paris (1976–). Has also conducted leading orchestras, including the Berlin Philharmonic, BBC Symphony and Concertgebouw, Amsterdam.

TALICH, Václav, b. 1883, Kromeriz, Bohemia; d. Brno, Czechoslovakia, 1961, After a career as a violinist, became a conductor, notably of Plzen Opera (1912–15). Administrator of National Opera, Prague (1935–45). Sacked in 1945, restored in 1947 and finally removed in 1948, being restored yet again in 1954.

TAUSKY, Vilem, b. 1910, Prerov, Czechoslovakia. Also a composer. National Opera, Brno (1929–39). After the war, he became Musical Director of Carl Rosa Opera (1945–49), also guest conducting at Covent Garden and Sadler's Wells. Best known for his work at the BBC (1951–) especially with the BBC Concert Orchestra. The Director of Opera at the Guildhall

School of Music and Drama, where his work has been widely admired.

TCHAKAROV, Emil, b. 1948, Bourgas, Bulgaria. Prizewinner at the 1971 Karajan Competition for Conducting. After many concert performances in North America, made his operatic debut at Plovidiv, Bulgaria, with *Tristan und Isolde*. Founded Sofia Festival Sinfonietta (1977). He has also conducted in Mexico, Japan etc. Debut at Covent Garden with *Eugene Onegin* (1979).

TCHEREPNIN, Nicolai, b. 1873, St. Petersburg, Russia; d. Issy-les-Moulineaux, France, 1945. Also a composer. Conductor of the Diaghilev company (1909–14).

TEMIRKANOV, Yuri, b. 1939, Nalchik, USSR. Originally a violinist, he became a conductor with the Leningrad Opera (1965). He won the Second National Conductors' Competition (the first had been thirty years earlier) in 1968. Musical Director, Leningrad Symphony Orchestra (1969–), touring with them to the USA, Germany, France, Italy, Japan, Sweden and elsewhere. Artistic Director and Chief Conductor, the

Kirov Opera, Leningrad (1977–).

A regular conductor of the Philadelphia in the 1970s, he has also conducted the Berlin Philharmonic, the Vienna Philharmonic etc. London debut with the Royal Philharmonic, the Vienna Philharmonic etc. London debut with the Royal Philharmonic (1977), since when he has appeared with the Philharmonia, City of Birmingham and Royal Liverpool Philharmonic Orchestras and is now (1979–) Principal Guest Conductor, Royal Philharmonic Orchestra.

TENNSTEDT, Klaus, b. 1926, Merseburg, Germany. A leading East German conductor until 1971, having conducted the Leipzig Gewandhaus, Berlin Symphony Orchestra etc. After working in Sweden, he became Generalmusikdirektor, Kiel Opera. A very successful guest conductor in North America (1974–), with annual performances at Tanglewood (1975–). Regularly conducts the London Philharmonic Orchestra. Chief Conductor, NDR Symphony Orchestra. Hamburg (1979–).

THOMAS, Theodore, b. 1835, Esens, Germany; d. Chicago, USA, 1905. Reaching the USA aged ten, he began as a violinist. He became America's leading conductor, founding the Chicago Symphony Orchestra (1891) and conducting it until he died. He had conducted the Theodore Thomas Orchestra in 1864 in New York with a well-paid, full-time personnel. In Chicago he had to endure salvoes of abuse from the Press and others, and, indeed, he was a tough autocrat, but he was America's first great conductor

and he raised orchestral standards, introduced a vast repertory, and helped to make his adopted country truly musical.

THOMPSON, Bryden, b. Ayr, Scotland. Since 1977, Conductor, Ulster Orchestra.

TIETJEN, Heinz, b. 1881, Tangier, Morocco; d. Baden-Baden, Germany, 1967. Also a producer. At Trier (1904–22) as conductor/producer, then at Saarbrucken and Breslau, Städitsche Oper, Berlin (1925–30). Generalintendant, Berlin, Preussisches Staatstheater (1927–45). Artistic Director, Bayreuth (1931–54), conducting the *Ring*, *Lohengrin* and *Meistersinger*. Intendant, Städitsche Oper, Berlin (1948–54). At Hamburg (1954–59), also working at Covent Garden (as producer) in the 1950s. Returned to Bayreuth (1958–59).

TIKKA, Kari, b. 1946, Siilinjarvi, Finland. Debut, Helsinki (1968), since when his posts have included National Opera, Helsinki (1970–72) and Swedish Royal Opera House (1975). He has also conducted in USSR, Poland and Germany.

TIMMS, Clive, b. 1946, Slough. Assistant Musical Director, English National Opera North (1979–).

TJEKNAVORIAN, Loris, b. 1937, Iran (of Armenian parentage). Also a composer. After being Composer in Residence, Ministry of Culture and Principal Conductor, Tehran Opera, he moved to London (1975), becoming an international conductor. Appears regularly with the London Symphony Orchestra and London Philharmonic Orchestras (1976–), and has toured Europe, US, Japan, South Africa etc.

TOSCANINI, Arturo, b. 1867, Parma, Italy; d. New York, USA, 1957. The most famous conductor of the century and an extraordinary, fiery personality, whose critics – and he had and has some fierce ones – have never denied his stature and overwhelming intensity of feeling for music. Originally a cellist, he took over the baton at a performance of *Aida* in Rio de Janeiro (1886) after the usual conductor had been subjected to a demonstration. Returning to Italy, he became a conductor, his premières in the '90s including *Pagliacci* (Milan, 1892) and *La Bohème* (Turin, 1892). At La Scala (1898–1902) as Principal Conductor. He was admired by Verdi (he had been in the pit as a cellist at the première of *Otello* in 1887). This was the first of his three reigns at La Scala, the others being 1906–08 and 1921–29.

Toscanini's first spell ended when he refused to allow Zenatello an encore in *Un Ballo in Maschera*, the second when he went to the Metropolitan, New York (1908–15) and the third when he fell out with the Fascists. These La Scala periods are generally regarded as the most glorious in the theatre's long history – the incomparable conductor with an extraordinarily gifted group of

Arturo Toscanini, the most famous conductor of modern times, with a personality to match.

singers. An autocrat, often a tyrant, his commitment to opera – *to the composer* – was total. As well as raising the standard of performance of Italian opera, he expanded the repertory to include many non-Italian works, including *Salome*, *Pelléas et Mélisande* and *Boris Godunov*. His premières included *Turandot* (1926) and he was a particular champion of Catalani, even naming his daughter Wally after the heroine of *La Wally*. As well as opera, he was giving symphony concerts in Italy from the early years of the century: they had been a rarity before his time. Debussy was one of his early favourites.

At the Metropolitan, his premières included *La Fanciulla del West* (1907) and the American première of *Boris*. He left probably because of lack of rehearsal time and the management's economies, also because of personal hostility to the Manager, Gatti-Casazza. His later engagements in opera were at Salzburg (1934–37), where his *Fidelio* and *Falstaff* remain operatic legends, and at Bayreuth (1930–31). Later, he conducted concert versions of opera for NBC in New York, some of which were released as recordings.

Toscanini first conducted the New York Philharmonic in 1926, was co-Conductor with Mengelberg (1927) and Principal Conductor of the merged Philharmonic and New York Symphony from 1928–36. The tough New York musicians were for once awed, and, we are told, those who had not worked with the terrible maestro were horrified at the prospect. Winthrop Sargent (a violinist before he became a critic) was to relate how every performance and rehearsal was made a continuous psychology of crisis by Toscanini, and how musicians would actually take their parts home and practise. He became Chief Conductor of the NBC Symphony Orchestra (created for him by NBC) in 1937. His fame was now colossal, reaching those who never went to concerts, while his rages were terrible to behold and to hear. They were in the service of the music and with the view of having every note played as written. Musical standards were raised not only by him but generally. The NBC's ensemble was astounding. The maestro conducted from memory, his eyesight being poor. Not all his recordings of this period do him justice because of a hard acoustic in the hall used, while his interpretations naturally attracted criticism as well as rapturous praise. His Beethoven was too 'perfect' and literal for some. But there are plenty of recordings, including music by Debussy and Verdi's *Requiem*, live from Carnegie Hall, and *Otello*, which remain as proof of his legend. He conducted little contemporary music, in his later years, for which he was criticised, but neither did many of his great contemporaries. His methods were copied by lesser men, who produced the notes as written without his burning intensity and vision, his awesome power.

Toscanini returned to Europe from time to time after the war, most notably to conduct at the reopening of La Scala (1946), which had been bombed and restored. His career ended on April 4, 1954, when he had a blackout in the middle of the

Baccanale from *Tannhäuser*. After much confusion, the broadcast concert continued. And that was the end.

TURNOVSKY, Martin, b. 1928, Prague, Czechoslovakia. Debut with Prague Symphony Orchestra (1952). State Philharmonic Orchestra, Brno (1960–63). Musical Director, Pilsen Radio Orchestra (1963–67). Dresden State Opera and State Orchestra (1967–68). He has also conducted the Radio Orchestra, Berlin, Cleveland Orchestra, Toronto Symphony Orchestra, Stockholm Philharmonic, Bournemouth Symphony Orchestra etc. Musical Director, Norwegian Opera, Oslo (1975–80).

URBANYI-KRASNODEBSKA, Zofia, b. 1936, Bydgoscz, Poland. Debut with Scout Symphony Orchestra, Warsaw Opera House (1959). A regular conductor of choirs and opera. Founded and conducted I Musici Cantani (1966–72).

VALACH, Jan, b. 1925, Hnusta, Czechoslovakia. Also an organist. Posts have included Conductor and Choral Director, National Opera Bratislava, Artistic Director, Opera House, Banska Bratislava, also Royal Opera House, Antwerp (1968). Arti Vocali, Antwerp (1974–).

VALEK, Vladimir, b. 1935, Nový Jičín, Czechoslovakia. Has conducted the leading Czech orchestras, also in USA, USSR, Italy and Germany.

VAN OTTERLOO, Jan, b. 1907, Winterswijk, Holland. Debut, Utrecht Civic Orchestra (1938). Chief Conductor, Hague Philharmonic Orchestra (1949–73), since when his posts have included Chief Conductor, Sydney Symphony Orchestra and Dusseldorf Symphoniker. Currently Musical Director, Sydney Symphony Orchestra.

VAN REMOORTEL, Edouard-William, b. 1926, Brussels, Belgium; d. Paris, 1977. Debut, Geneva (1945). Musical Director and Permanent Conductor, St. Louis Symphony Orchestra (1958–62), after which engagements included Principal Guest Conductor, Orquestra Sinfónica Nacional of Mexico.

VANDERNOOT, André, b. 1927, Brussels, Belgium. Musical Director, Orchestre National de Belgique (1954). Toured Europe with Vienna Symphony Orchestra (1955). Conducted in Berlin, Vienna, Warsaw, London, Paris etc. First Conductor, Theatre Royal de la Monnaie, Brussels (1960).

VAN der STUCKEN, Frank, b. 1858, Fredericksburg, Texas; d. Hamburg, Germany 1929. Also a composer. Studied in Antwerp and Leipzig, returning home to become an orchestral and choral conductor. Cincinnati Symphony Orchestra (1895–1907). One of the first native American conductors, though he spent his later life in Germany.

VANZO, Vittorio, b. 1862, Padua, Italy; d. Milan, 1945. Also a composer. Gave the first Italian *Walkure* (Turin, 1891) and *Götterdämmerung* (La Scala, 1897).

VARVISO, Silvio, b. 1924, Zurich, Switzerland. Basel (1950–58), Musical Director from 1956. Guest conductor

Berlin Staatsoper (1958–61), San Francisco Opera (1959–61). Metropolitan, New York (1962: 1968–69). Glyndebourne (1962–63), and regularly at Covent Garden (1961–). Musical Director, Royal Opera, Stockholm (1965–72). Generalmusikdirektor, Stuttgart (1972–). Bayreuth (1969–74). This distinguished conductor is to be Musical Director, Paris Opéra (1981–).

VASARY, Tamas, b. 1933, Debrecen, Hungary. This great pianist is beginning to conduct regularly. Co-Conductor, Northern Sinfonia (1979–).

VAUGHAN, Denis, b. 1926, Melbourne, Australia. Also harpsichordist and musicologist. Posts include Assistant Conductor/Chorus Master with Beecham (1954–57). Musical Director, State Opera, South Australia (1981–).

VAUGHAN WILLIAMS, Ralph, b. 1872, Down Ampney, England; d. London, 1958. The much-loved composer was also a fine conductor, especially of choral music.

VELTRI, Michelangelo, b. Buenos Aires, Argentina. After conducting at the Teatro Colon, Buenos Aires, in the 1960s, he went to Stuttgart (1965), also Italy, since when he has conducted concerts and opera in Europe and America.

VERBRUGGHEN, Henri, b. 1873, Brussels, Belgium; d. Northfield, Minnesota, USA, 1934. Originally a violinist, he became leader of the Scottish Orchestra and founded a string quartet, which moved to Sydney, Australia. Conductor of the Minneapolis Orchestra (1922–32).

VIVIENNE, Hazel, b. 1934, Bromborough, England. Chorus Master, English National Opera (1964–76), conducting the Company regularly (1967–). Head of Music Staff (1975–).

VONK, Hans, b. 1942, Amsterdam, Holland. Principal Conductor, Residentie Orchestra, the Hague, also Radio Philharmonic Orchestra, Hilversum.

WAART, Edo de, b. 1941, Amsterdam, Holland. Won the Mitropoulos prize, 1964. Musical Director and Principal Conductor, Rotterdam Philharmonic Orchestra (1975–), touring with the orchestra in the USA, Britain, Germany and Austria. San Francisco Symphony Orchestra (1975–). He has also conducted many of the world's leading orchestras. Operatic debut with Netherlands Opera (1970), which he has often conducted. Covent Garden debut, *Ariadne auf Naxos* (1976). He has also conducted opera at Santa Fé, Houston and the Holland Festival.

WAGNER, Richard, b. 1813, Leipzig, Germany; d. Venice, Italy, 1883. As the 'strongest conducting force of the century' (Harold Schonberg), the great composer is discussed in Chapters 1 and 3.

WALLENSTEIN, Alfred, b. 1898, Chicago, USA. Originally a cellist with the New York Philharmonic. The only native-born conductor of his day to be appointed to a major orchestra, the Los Angeles Philharmonic (1943–56). A regular broadcaster on music, and conductor of Symphony of the Air 1961–63.

WALLENSTEIN, Lothar, b. 1882, Prague, Bohemia; d. New Orleans, USA, 1949. Also a producer. Conductor at Poznan (1910–14), where he also produced. He later turned almost entirely to production, in Germany, Italy, South America and at the Metropolitan (1941–46).

WALTER, Bruno, b. 1876, Berlin, Germany; d. Los Angeles, USA, 1962. Also a composer. This great conductor, adored by musicians and public alike, believed in the spiritual values of music. Art was a sacrament to him and music was a moral force; indeed he wrote a book called *On Moral Forces of Music*. His warm, relaxed, romantic readings of German and Austrian music, added to his intense musicianship, made him the idol of many opera and concertgoers.

His posts included Hamburg (1894–96), Breslau, Pressburg, Riga, Berlin and then Vienna (1901–12), first as Mahler's assistant. Mahler's influence on him was colossal and he was to give the first performance of the 9th Symphony and *Das Lied von der Erde* (1911). He was Generalmusikdirektor at Munich (1913–22) owing to the sudden death of Mottl, and his premières included Pfitzner's *Palestrina*

(1917). At Berlin Staatsoper (1925–29), also Generalmusikdirektor, Vienna (1936–38). He conducted regularly at the Metropolitan, New York (1941–59) and at Covent Garden (1924–31), though not, alas, after the war. He also conducted the Berlin Philharmonic and the New York Philharmonic, becoming an American citizen (having been forced to flee from the Nazis as a Jew). He appeared again in Britain and Europe after the war. He was one of the finest modern conductors of Mozart, seeing him as 'the Shakespeare of the opera' and not merely a rococo composer, as some maintained a generation ago.

WANGENHEIM, Volker, b. 1928, Berlin, Germany. Also a composer. Chief Conductor, Berlin Mozart Orchestra (1950–59). Conductor, Mecklenburg State Opera, Schwerin (1951–52). Appointed Music Director of the City of Bonn (1957) since when much of his career has been as a leading figure in Bonn music. Principal Conductor, Bournemouth Sinfonietta (1978–).

WANTANABE, Akeo, b. 1919, Tokyo, Japan. Musical Director and Permanent Conductor, Tokyo Metropolitan Symphony Orchestra (1972–), taking the orchestra on a European tour in 1977. He has also been a guest conductor in Britain, Canada, Finland and elsewhere, and has been given a Finnish award for introducing Finnish music to Japan.

WEBER, Carl Maria von, b. 1786, Eutin, Germany; d. London 1826. The great German composer was also one of the first great conductors, and is discussed as such in Chapters 1 and 3.

WEINGARTNER, Felix, b. 1863, Zara, Dalmatia; d. Winterhur, Switzerland, 1942. Also a composer and pianist (a student of Liszt). After being Kapellmeister at Königsberg (1884–85) and Danzig (1885–87), he went to Hamburg (1877–89), where his *Carmen* was a challenge to Bülow, whom he considered dragged the opera. Indeed, he attacked Bülow's excessive romanticism generally. He next went to Mannheim (1889–91), Berlin (1891–98), Vienna (1908–11), taking over from Mahler. He was at Hamburg again (1912–14), Darmstadt (1915–19), the Vienna Volksoper (1919–24) and the State Opera (1935–36) and he also conducted in Boston and at Covent Garden. However, he is not primarily remembered as an operatic

Felix Weingartner, whose Beethoven performances were – and remain – legendary.

conductor: for many, he lacked drama. He also riled many in Vienna who had served the incomparable Mahler, and he cut Wagner.

Weingartner's symphonic career was triumphant. As Conductor of the Berlin Hofkappelle (1891–1902) and the Vienna Philharmonic Orchestra (1908–27), and as a regular guest conductor elsewhere – he conducted in Britain from 1898–1940 – his performances of Beethoven were and remain a legend, while his book on performing the symphonies (1906) became a standard work. Interestingly, his performances did not vary down the years (as records prove). His reputation remains secure and colossal.

WELLER, Walter, b. 1939, Vienna, Austria. Also a violinist: he founded the Weller Quartet in 1958. Conductor at the Vienna State Opera (1969–). Royal Liverpool Philharmonic Orchestra (1979). Principal Conductor, Royal Philharmonic Orchestra (1980–).

WELTER, Horst, b. 1914, Frankfurt, Germany. A pupil of Hindemith, he has held a number of posts in Germany, including Karlsruhe and Wilhelmshaven, and has conducted in many parts of Europe. He made his London debut with the Royal Philharmonic Orchestra (1977).

WIERSZYLOWSKI, Jan, b. 1927, Jablonna, Poland. As well as regularly conducting the Warsaw National Philharmonic Orchestra, he is a teacher and an expert in old music, especially Polish music.

WILLCOCKS, (Sir) David, b. 1919, Newquay, England. Particularly famous for his long spell at his old college, King's Cambridge, where he was Fellow and Director of Music (1957–73). Music Director of Bach Choir (1960–) and Director of the Royal College of Music (1974–). He has made a vast number of recordings. Knighted in 1977.

WILLIAMS, John b. 1932, New York, USA. The internationally famous composer of film music has succeeded the late Arthur Fiedler as Conductor of the Boston Pops.

WOLFF, Albert, b. 1884, Paris, France; d. Paris 1970. Also a composer. Conducted at Opéra-Comique, Paris (1911–34). At Metropolitan, New York (1919–21). Musical Director of Opéra-Comique (1921–24) and Theatre Director (1945–46). He also conducted Concerts Lamoureux in Paris.

WOOD, (Sir) Henry, b. 1869, London, England; d. Hitchin, England, 1944. His long and supremely fruitful association with the Promenade Concerts that bear his name make him one of the most important figures in Britain's musical history, and his life is a reminder that achievement can be even more significant than greatness – for no one has ranked him as a great conductor. He was a very good one and an inspired teacher of orchestras, choral societies and singers.

His early career was in opera. He made his debut with the Arthur Rouseby Opera Co. (1889), assisted

The young Henry Wood conducted his first Prom in 1895 and his last 50 years later – as Sir Henry.

Sullivan with his opera *Ivanhoe* (1890), and other operatic work included conducting the first British *Eugene Onegin* in London (1892). In 1895, he was engaged by Robert Newman to conduct a series of Promenade Concerts at the Queen's Hall, London, and he was to conduct his last Prom on 18 July 1944, shortly before his death. It was his 50th Prom season, the concerts having been transferred to the Albert Hall after the bombing of the Queen's Hall (1941). Not until 1939 did he share his colossal work load with another conductor, Basil Cameron. His Queen's Hall Orchestra and, later, the BBC Symphony Orchestra would (until 1942) play every concert for eight or more weeks. No concerts did more to spread a love of orchestral music in Britain, much new music included, especially after broadcasting of them began in the 1930s. Wood was particularly successful in popularizing Russian music. Also popular, though not with musical scholars, were his transcriptions of Handel, Bach etc. His players called him Timber or Old Timber, not just a play on his name, but a tribute to his sterling qualities. His Queen's Hall orchestra was the first truly permanent one in Britain, being founded in 1895 for the Proms and other concerts. He challenged the system whereby players sent deputies to rehearsals, or even performances. Some of those who rebelled against him formed the London Symphony Orchestra (1904). He worked miracles with too few rehearsals for year after year and was a welcome guest conductor in Europe and America. Despite the fact that each left the other out of their autobiographies he and Beecham in their very different ways did more than anyone else – along with a handful of composers – to banish the legend of Britain as a Land without Music.

WOOLDRIDGE, David, b. 1931, Deal, England. Also a composer. Staff Conductor Bavarian State Opera (1954–55), Music Director, Beirut

Symphony Orchestra (1961–65) and a wide-ranging guest conductor. The author of *The Conductor's World* (1969).

WORDSWORTH, Barry. b. 1948, London. Principal Conductor, Sadler's Wells Royal Ballet (1979–).

WOSS, Kurt, b. 1925, Linz, Austria. Conducted the Vienna Symphony Orchestra aged twenty-two becoming Permanent Conductor, Tonkunstler-Orchester, Vienna (1947). Chief Conductor, Japanese Broadcasting Orchestra (1951–53). Resident Conductor, Victorian Symphony Orchestra, Melbourne (1956–60), with many guest performances in Europe, the USA and elsewhere.

WRIGHT, Brian, b. 1946, Tonbridge, England. Debut, Royal Festival Hall, London, *Messiah* (1972). Has conducted leading British orchestras. Assistant Conductor, London Symphony Orchestra (1974–75). Conductor, BBC Choral Society (1976–). Gave first complete London performance of Liszt's *Christus* with the Royal Philharmonic (1977). Has conducted in Belgium, Germany, Portugal, Switzerland etc.

WÜLLNER, Franz, b. 1832, Munster, Germany; d. Braunfels, 1902. Also a composer. Successor to Bülow at Munich Court Theatre (1869). Coped with the difficulties surrounding the first *Rheingold* (1869) and *Walküre* (1870) – so well that he became Court Kapellmeister-in-Chief (1870). Berlin Philharmonic (1883–84) Director of Cologne Conservatoire (1884), where he gave the first performance of Strauss's *Till Eulenspiegel* (1895) and *Don Quixote* (1897).

YADYKH, Pavel, b. 1927, Vinnitsa, Ukraine, USSR. Debut: State Symphony Orchestra of USSR, Kiev. Conductor-in-Chief, N-Ossetia Symphony Orchestras, and conducts leading orchestras all over Russia, also opera.

YUASA, Takuob, b. Osaka, Japan. Debut with Tonkunstler Orchestra in Vienna (1976). With Kyoto Symphony Orchestra (1977), then other leading Japanese orchestras. Nikikai Opera, Osaka (1978–), where he also promotes Japanese operas.

ZANINELLI, Luigi, b. 1932, Raritan, New Jersey, USA. Also a composer. Debut, Juilliard School of Music (1951). Much of his career has been in TV and radio. Producer-Director, CBS-TV series of 20th century music.

ZDRAVKOVITCH, Gika, b. 1914, Belgrade, Yugoslavia. Musical Director, Belgrade Philharmonic Orchestra, and has conducted in many countries in Europe, Asia, America and Africa, also on TV and radio.

ZENDER, Johannes, b. 1936, Weisbaden, Germany. Also a composer. Posts include Principal Conductor, Bonn (1964). Principal Conductor, Saar Broadcasting (1971–). Has conducted at Bayreuth, Munich, Hamburg, Cologne etc.

ZOEPHEL, Klaus, b. 1929, Plauen/ Vogtland, East Germany. Also a composer. Posts include: Musical Director, National Theatre, Weimar (1957–61) and Musical Director, State Cultural Orchestra, Mulhausen (1962–63).

ZOLLMAN, Ronald, b. 1950, Antwerp, Belgium. Conductor of many Belgian orchestras, including Orchestre Nationale de Belgique.

ZUMPE, Hermann, b. 1850, Taubenheim, Germany; d. Munich, 1903. Also a composer. Bayreuth (1873–76), after which his many posts included Hamburg (1884–86), Stuttgart (1891–95) and Munich (1900–03).

The Founding Fathers

It is hard to imagine anyone successfully challenging Harold Schonberg's statement that Berlioz, Mendelssohn and Wagner are the trinity upon which all modern conducting is based. It seems appropriate therefore to provide a number of significant quotations by or about them to add to what was written about them in Chapter 1. To begin with, however, three of their most important predecessors are featured.

First, here is Weber writing fascinatingly to a Leipzig friend of his named Praeger. Weingartner quoted it in his book *On Conducting*:

> The tempo must not be like a tyrannical hammer, holding up or urging on, but must be to the music what the pulse-beat is to a man's life.
>
> There is no slow tempo without passages that demand a faster motion, so as to prevent the impression of dragging. On the other hand there is no *presto* that does not need a soft delivery in many places, so as not to lose the opportunity of expressiveness by undue haste.
>
> But from what I have said, for heaven's sake let no singer think himself justified in using that lunatic style of phrasing which consists in the capricious distortion of isolated bars, giving the listener the same unbearably painful sensation as the sight of a juggler violently straining all his limbs. Neither the speeding up nor the slowing down of the tempo should ever suggest the spasmodic or the violent. For the changes to have a musical-poetic significance, they must come in an orderly fashion in periods and phrases, occasioned by the varying warmth of expression.
>
> We have no signs in music for all this. They only exist in the perceptive human soul; if they are not present, there can be

no help from the metronome – which gets rid of only the more gross errors – nor from my very imperfect maxims, which, when considering the size of the subject, I might be tempted to develop them much more fully, were I not warned by unhappy experiences how superfluous and worthless they are and how likely to be misunderstood.

We now come to Spontini, already characterized by the German musician, Moritz Hanemann, in Chapter 1. Hanemann revealed that the Napoleon of the orchestra could actually be polite, for though the great man stood 'like a bronze statue' and inspired the fear of God in his players, at the end he always said: 'I thank you.'

An English visitor, who saw Spontini in action in Berlin in 1829, wrote about him in the magazine *Harmonicon*. Spontini was seated 'close to the stage with his back to the audience: and as he only follows the score and marks the time, there is produced that unity of effect which so much distinguishes the operatic performances on the continent.'

The English visitor was no lover of Spontini the man:

> Spontini, though standing very high as a composer, is not personally a favourite: he bears himself toward everyone with a hauteur and repulsiveness of manner totally unworthy of a man of genius.

Eduard Devrient was not such an admirer of Spontini as a musician. Devrient was one of the famous family of German actors of that name, though he had started out as a singer, and was a close friend and warm admirer of Mendelssohn, the very opposite type of conductor and personality to Spontini. He wrote that the 'ministry of Spontini' in Berlin was:

> ... a period of false splendour, ruinous to the spirit of German music, of which Spontini had not an idea. The violent contrasts in which he sought his effects, the startling shocks of his *sforzati*, in fact all his effects, calculated to tell only on the nerves and senses of his listeners, could not but demoralize his orchestra. To this was added that the perfect precision and control for which his conducting was famous, ceased when he no longer held the baton.

This leads us to Devrient's friend Mendelssohn, that delightful man and perfect musician. Naturally, he described his friend in action:

> Felix was calm and collected in his difficult post as though he had already conducted a dozen festivals. The quiet simple way in which he by a look, a movement of the head or hand, reminded us of the inflections agreed upon, and thus ruled every phrase; the confidence with which he would drop his baton during the longer movements, when he knew they were safe, with a little nod as much as to say, 'this will go very well without me' – listen with radiant countenance, occasionally glancing towards me – in all he was as great as he was lovable.

That was the composer-conductor aged twenty, conducting the first revival of Bach's *St. Matthew Passion* in Leipzig in 1829.

Many of Mendelssohn's admirers went even further, though he does not seem to have been so successful away from his Gewandhaus orchestra in Leipzig, except when he was conducting his own works. His liking for quick tempos resulted in a number of listeners finding the results superficial in some of his Beethoven performances. Wagner, a very different sort of conductor, recalled that Mendelssohn had said to him:

> ... with regard to conducting, that he thought most harm was done by taking a *tempo* too slow; and that on the contrary, he always recommended quick *tempi* as being less detrimental. Really good execution, he thought, was at all times a rare thing, but shortcomings might be disguised if care was taken that they should not appear very prominent; and the best way to do this was *to get over the ground very quickly*.

Otto Nicolai deserves a place in this impressive roster of composer-conductors. The composer of *The Merry Wives of Windsor* and founder of the Vienna Philharmonic Orchestra was a conductor who drew these words from Hector Berlioz:

> I regard him as one of the best orchestral leaders I have ever met. He is one of those men whose influence alone suffices to bestow a marked musical superiority on the town in which they live, when provided with the necessary opportunities. He

possesses three qualities indispensable to a finished conductor. He is a learned composer, skilled and enthusiastic, he has a strong feeling for rhythm, and his mode of conducting is perfectly clear and exact; in short, he is an ingenious and indefatigable organizer, grudging neither time nor trouble at rehearsals; one who knows what he is doing because he only does what he knows. Hence the excellent qualities, moral and material, the confidence, devotion, patience, marvellous assurance and unity of action of the *Kärntnerthor* orchestra.

Nicolai was fortunate in securing enough rehearsals for major events. For his historic performance of Beethoven's Ninth in Vienna in 1843, the first great performance of the work, he had thirteen rehearsals.

Berlioz, arguably the greatest of French composers, was undoubtedly a very great conductor, and far less sober than his chapter on conducting in his *Instrumentation* suggests. He cannot in performance have been quite so exact and steady in his tempo, quite so lacking in rubato, even though he was clearly less prone to flexibility than Wagner, whose opinion of him has been noted in Chapter 1.

Considering that in any generation there are only a handful of conductors whom true Berliozians consider can interpret the master, it is hardly surprising that Berlioz ran into trouble himself when confronted with players almost invariably inferior to today's, and quite unable to comprehend his unique musical vision, a vision that eludes many music lovers to this day. Sir Charles Hallé thought the world of Berlioz's conducting, which is pleasing not only in itself, but also because one of his greatest successors with the Hallé Orchestra was the leading Berliozian of his day, Sir Hamilton Harty. Hallé recalled the Berlioz of 1837:

> And what a picture he was at the head of his orchestra, with his eagle face, his bushy hair, his air of command, and glowing with enthusiasm. He was the most perfect conductor that I ever set eyes upon, one who held absolute sway over his troops, and played upon them as a pianist upon the keyboard.

There is no doubt that Berlioz's beat remained precise and clear even at the most volcanic moments. Not for him a musical diet of rubato. The arch romantic was also an arch classicist, as his admirers know, so it was inevitable that his conducting reflected this. The beat might be precise, but, as Anton Seidl told Cosima Wagner:

> Now he was up in the air, then under the music desk; now he turned uneasily to the big drummer, then he was coaxing the flautist; now he was drawing out the tone from the violins, then stabbing through the air at the double-basses, or extracting a cantilena of love-yearning from the violoncellos. The musicians were rather afraid of this demoniac sarcastic face and struggled to escape his clutches.

And just as Berlioz the composer has had more success away from his native France, so Berlioz the conductor often had more success abroad.

Wagner, of course, was being welcomed abroad (as well as being execrated), his admirers including Queen Victoria and Prince Albert at a time he was *persona non grata* at home.

He is a phenomenon in the history of the performing arts. There is no other example of a great composer, great theatre director, inspired teacher of singers to act, (which, admittedly, is part of the job of the Director, though too few can do it) and highly effective playwright. If he had not had the misfortune to live at a time when theatre design in Germany was at a very low ebb, he would have been an even greater artistic phenomenon. As it was, the first *Ring* in 1876 was a visual disappointment. That Wagner was a great conductor, however, is beyond question.

The child of Weber, whom he worshipped, he wanted total musical theatre. We are only concerned here with Wagner the conductor, and a mighty one he was. As has been noted more than once, he believed in a flexible tempo. His inspiration, operatically and musically, was the incomparable singer-actress, Schröder-Devrient, whose Fidelio had an immense effect; for she was a creative artist, like Callas, and like Callas, her voice finally failed to uphold her vision.

A tempo, Wagner believed, should vary depending on the emotional nature of the melody. Anton Seidl put it very clearly when he said that it was the phrase, the melody, the expression, that ruled Wagner's conducting, not the time beat.

Wagner being Wagner, he could not always achieve his ideals as a conductor, but he was certainly the father of the conductor as we know him, unless one considers Hans von Bülow as that father and Wagner as the grandfather. Incredibly, he was a poor score reader and did not play an instrument. And his conducting was not helped by his personality. Such a man amongst men was inevitably a super-egoist.

Wagner's friend Praeger of Leipzig stated:

> Wagner does not beat in the old-fashioned automato-metronomic manner. He leaves off beating at times – then resumes again – to lead the orchestra up to a climax, or to let them soften down to a pianissimo, as if a thousand invisible threads tied them to his baton.

Hanslick, immortalized as Beckmesser the critic in *Meistersinger*, was notoriously no champion of Wagner, though a very notable critic. An appreciation of Wagner the conductor in 1863 is a paean of praise, beginning with, 'He is an excellent conductor, full of spirit and fire.'

Wagner was less lucky in London in 1855, not least because he had too few rehearsals, but also because he was not Mendelssohn, being very outspoken and impatient; also he could not speak English. Naturally, most of the critics had a field day at his expense, and, indeed, he was not seen and heard at his best. Yet the critic of the *Illustrated London News* was aware of his worth:

> His appearance at the head of the Philharmonic band enabled the public to judge only of one thing – his capacity as a *chef d'orchestre*; a point which that one evening settled beyond all question. Though the whole orchestra – till the rehearsal two days before – were utter strangers to him, yet that single rehearsal had established so thoroughly an understanding between them, that, at the concert, every piece was performed with a clearness, spirit, and delicacy which we have never heard surpassed: and this was the more remarkable, as his manner of marking the time, and his reading of many passages, differed materially from those of his predecessor ... So convinced were the audience of the admirable manner in which he had acquitted himself that at the conclusion of the concert, he was saluted with repeated rounds of applause.

The great violinist Joachim, no hard core Wagnerian, either as artist or man, characterized him as a conductor as having a lively sense of the music he was conducting and the gift of imparting it to his players, of whom he was the master. Joachim then lamented that Wagner was not as modest as he was capable. For which many thanks ...

Let the last word of this short appendix on a large subject be with a staunch Wagnerian, the conductor Seidl. In the midst of a panegyric, he proclaimed:

> Under his direction the weakest orchestra grew strong and played gloriously; their tone acquired life and expressiveness, the strictest rhythm and the most sublime expression of feeling conquered, and the whole was reflected in Wagner's face. Everybody hung on his look, he seemed to be looking at everybody at the same moment.

Not for the first time in this book the eyes have it.

Select Discography

A PERSONAL CHOICE

Rather than provide the mere list of titles and numbers that is often to be found at the back of music books and rather than compete with entire books on the subject of recordings, here is a selection of just ten, with brief notes on each. Four of the ten different conductors are from the past. Fortunately, considering what has been written earlier about their different, but equally valid, approach to the conductor's art, Toscanini and Furtwängler are two of the four. Klemperer is another, and the fourth is Beecham, the joker in the pack, who could – to put it mildly – be capricious on occasion, yet who at his best was incomparable. The Toscanini, Beecham and Furtwängler recordings are widely regarded as landmarks in gramophone history, and they, like the Klemperer recording are all available at the time of writing. The other choices are not indisputable landmarks, though many may consider them so, but all are exceptionally fine performances. To avoid trying to list the ten in order of merit the conductors' dates of birth dictate the running order. No composer has been allowed to appear twice, otherwise Giulini's *Don Carlos* and Goodall's and Solti's *Rings*, or parts of them, might have been included.

ARTURO TOSCANINI: *Requiem Mass* by Verdi. With Herva Nelli, Fedora Barbieri Giuseppe di Stefano, Cesare Siepi, the NBC Symphony Orchestra and the Robert Shaw Chorale. Recorded at a broadcast performance in Carnegie Hall, January 27, 1951. LPAT 201.

Toscanini's colossal reputation, a mixed one towards the end of his own lifetime, can in the last resort rest secure because of this performance and his recording of Verdi's *Otello*. Both are legendary interpretations of masterpieces, yet perhaps because it was recorded live, the *Requiem* seems even more electrifying than the opera. The audience noises can be heard, but are not obtrusive.

Superlatives are apt to become monotonous in the face of such glories as are on display here, so let it simply be noted that three out of four of the soloists were inspired by Toscanini to excel themselves, and the fourth, the soprano Nelli, manage to survive in such exalted company. Di Stefano in 1951 had the voice of a young god. Let there never come a time when this epic recording is deleted from the catalogue.

SIR THOMAS BEECHAM: *Die Zauberflöte* by Mozart. SH 157–60. Cast includes Tiana Lemnitz as Pamina, Erna Berger as the Queen of the Night, Helge Roswaenge as Tamino, Gerhard Hüsch as Papageno and Wilhelm Strienz as Sarastro. With the Berlin Philharmonic Orchestra. LP: SH 158–60.

Recorded in 1937–38, this version of the opera has surely never been surpassed. Beecham perhaps excelled in Mozart above all other composers. This venerable recording has no trace of a studio-bound performance. Instead it is heart-lifting, vigorous, meltingly beautiful, theatrical and profound, capturing the very spirit of this strange and ravishing masterpiece. Orchestra and soloists rise to Beecham's demands and the results are spellbinding. Only one performance, the Papageno, is as matchless as the overall conception, though Roswaenge's Tamino is passionate and vivid, if more weighty than the usual vocal characterization. Even Beecham's later *Die Entführung aus dem Serail* is not quite so perfect as this his finest tribute to his beloved Mozart.

OTTO KLEMPERER: Symphony No. 3 in E flat major, 'Eroica', by Beethoven. With the Philharmonia Orchestra, (also *Fidelio* Overture). 1962.

The long list of Eroicas recordings includes a roster of glory from 1947 (de Sabata with his beloved LPO) to the astounding 1979 version by Giulini and the Los Angeles Philharmonic. This presents what appears to be a classically severe, slow and almost Spartan first movement which yet grows more convincing with each hearing.

Yet for me Klemperer remains supreme. Some have claimed his earlier mono version even finer, yet surely the Funeral March in the 1962 performance, with its desolating ending, has never been equalled on disc. It is majestically heroic and sublimely, intensely tragic. The first movement is spacious, monumental and fiercely felt, for all that it is less obviously fiery and dramatic than many a faster version. As so often with Klemperer at his greatest, everything seems 'right'. This is not to say others are wrong, but that with Klemperer we glimpse Beethoven's vision. The third movement, with ravishing horns, leads to more grandeur and unhurried glory in the finale, with a glorious statement of mighty, sublime power at the end.

Re-released HMV Concert Classics, LP: SXLP 30310; Cassette TC-SXLP 30310, but recently withdrawn from the catalogue. May it return ...

WILHELM FURTWÄNGLER: *Tristan und Isolde* by Wagner. With Kirsten Flagstad as Isolde, Blanche Thebom as Brangaene, Ludwig Suthhaus as Tristan, Dietrich Fischer-Dieskau as Kurwenal and Josef Griendel as King Mark. Covent Garden Chorus. Philharmonia Orchestra. LP: RLS 684.

Every performance of *Tristan* is an event, and there are never many because it is so hard to cast adequately. Similarly, there have not been many complete recordings. At the time of writing, there is Karajan's captivatingly beautiful performance with the Berlin Philharmonic, with Dernesch surpassing herself as Isolde and with Jon Vickers, the finest Tristan of our day; Solti's highly charged performance with Nilsson in stupendous voice and magnificent in her artistry; Böhm's live Bayreuth performance, with Windgassen and Nilsson, which, despite splendours, is not in the same league; and there is Furtwängler's ...

There are few recordings of anything that have such fervent devotees as this one, and it is hardly surprising. It dates from 1953, and a typical reaction is Edmund Tracey's, when reviewing the 1965-re-issue for *Opera* magazine (Feb. 1966). Having stated soberly that the Philharmonia's playing 'beggars all description', he finished by confessing: 'Speechless with rapture, like the lovers themselves, I sink down by my electrostatic speakers, unable to say more.'

This recording is surely Furtwängler's greatest memorial, one that will never be allowed to disappear from the catalogue, and one that illustrates what has been said about him in this book and far more fully elsewhere. Wagner's own fluctuations of tempos have been noted in this book and Furtwängler was in the royal line of Wagnerian conducting. Faced with the blazing intensity of his vision, that 'sense of mystical removal, rather than mere erotic ecstacy', as Peter Heyworth said of Reginald Goodall's great *Tristan* for the Welsh National Opera, it is easy to imagine the hypnotic effect that the conductor had on his players, his audiences – and himself. For the record, Flagstad excels herself in one of her two greatest roles, and Suthaus, a lesser artist, is yet raised to notable stature in such glorious company.

GEORGE SZELL: Symphony No 4. in G major by Mahler. With Judith Raskin and the Cleveland Orchestra. LP: 61056; Cassette 40–61056.

I came to Mahler the composer long after revering his feats as Conductor and Director of the Vienna State Opera. This recording was the turning point. Dating back to 1967, it outstrips all its rivals, even the stunning 1975 one by James Levine and the Chicago Symphony Orchestra. In a performance of relaxed beauty and restrained virtuosity, Szell and his players, along with an ideal soprano soloist, provide a classic interpretation. The slow movement has a depth of emotion and nobility which no other recording can match. By any standards this must be one of the handful of ultimate Mahler performances to rank alongside Barbirolli's Fifth, Solti's Eighth and Haitink's Ninth, especially the Barbirolli, which remains one of the living proofs of his total affinity with a composer he came to late in life. But the die is cast ...

JOSEF KRIPS: *Symphony No. 9* in C major (The Great) by Schubert. With the London Symphony Orchestra. LP: SPA467; Cassette KCSP 467.

This is not simply chosen to celebrate a supreme hero of my early concert-going, which Krips was, and which shows in the Introduction to this book. It is perhaps the very finest performance on record of one of the most lyrical works in the whole symphonic repertoire. Originally released in 1959, it returned in 1977, hopefully never to disappear. Krips was one of the supreme guardians of the Viennese tradition, some might say *the* supreme guardian, for he had to rebuild the Vienna State Opera after the war. It should be noted that the *Penguin Cassette Guide* states that the cassette of the performance is not up to the excellent standard of the record, which is unfortunate for the growing number of cassette buyers, among whom I number myself.

There are many rivals to this recording, among them superb ones by Böhm and Haitink, yet for sheer spontaneous lyricism, none of them touches the playing of the LSO under Krips. The late William McNaught noted that this is the least argumentative of symphonies and that the music is simply enjoying itself. By this token, Krips's is the most enjoyable, the most heady, performance of them all.

HERBERT VON KARAJAN: *La Mer* by Debussy; *Prelude à l'àpres-midi d'un faune* by Debussy; *Daphnis et Chloë*: Suite No. 2 by Ravel. The Berlin Philharmonic Orchestra. LP: 138 923; Cassette 923–075.

Though von Karajan and his orchestra have recorded *La Mer* since, this 1965 version seems even truer to the spirit of the masterpiece than the later one, while the other two pieces are also given stunning performances. There are many rival recordings of *La Mer*, the finest surely being Giulini's and Stokowski's, pace Boulez enthusiasts, but neither seem atmospherically so right. The same may be said of the perfection of the *Daphnis and Chloë* suite, which has no rival, so matchlessly, convincingly and poetically does the great orchestra play for their extraordinary chief. One can only hope that, despite the growing number of new recordings of all three works – for the *Prelude* as well is ravishingly played – it will not disappear. It deserves to become a standard.

COLIN DAVIS: *Les Troyens* by Berlioz. 6709 002; Cassette (highlights) 7300 050. With Jon Vickers as Aeneas, Josephine Veasey as Dido, Berit Lindhold as Cassandra, Heather Begg as Anna, and the Orchestra and Chorus of the Royal Opera House, Covent Garden and the Wandsworth Boys' Choir.

I made my feelings clear about Colin Davis as a Berliozian in the last paragraph of Chapter 1 of this book, and again in the entry on him in the Who's Who section. This recording is the crowning achievement of his complete Berlioz cycle, which is not to say that it is necessarily the most perfect, for it is not, some of the cast being less than first rate. But *Les Troyens* is Berlioz's grandest and, for many, his greatest work, and it finds Davis at the very peak of his powers.

It is really two operas. The first part, *La Prise de Troie*, is Berlioz at his most classical for all its passion, a salute to Gluck as well as Virgil. The second part, *Les Troyens à Carthage*, is the very pinnacle of Romance. The whole is as wide-ranging as Shakespeare's *Henry IV*: Davis has always shown his monumental grasp of the masterpiece. The excitement of his reading is intense and never less than dramatic, the thrilling rhythmic vitality marvellously projecting the composer's unique, sometimes broken, sometimes lingering, so often ravishing melodies. Davis never fails to project the 'rightness' of Berlioz's frequently disputed musical ideas, while passages of sombre splendour never become mere rhetoric.

By the cruellest luck, Jon Vickers, an incomparable Aeneas, was not in the very best of health when the recording was made, so strain occasionally shows despite the sheer greatness of his characterization, musically and dramatically. Space forbids a discussion of the rest of the cast, for it is the conductor who is under consideration. This recording came out in 1970, just after the celebrations to commemorate the 100th anniversary of Berlioz's death. It was the worthiest of all tributes to the frustrated, tormented genius who composed this sublime epic. Shamefully, it is currently only available in highlights form (6500 161).

ANDRÉ PREVIN: *A London Symphony* by Vaughan Williams, with the London Symphony Orchestra. LP: SB 6860; Cassette RK 6860.

Because a third of my writing is devoted to American history in general and the American West in particular, I had originally planned to select Bernstein's electrifying recording of Copland's *Rodeo* and *Billy the Kid*, plus the four *Dance episodes*, (72411), which would also have been a tribute to the latter day Renaissance Man who gave us *Candide* and *West Side Story*. However, patriotism will out, even if it should have no place in the arts.

Previn's recording of the *London Symphony*, which dates from 1972, seems even finer, if such a thing is possible, than Sir Adrian Boult's 1971 version, perhaps because Previn's account of the work is slightly more dramatic and never a shade over-relaxed. (Alas, the cassette is less fine than the record.) Previn's love affair with English music is famous. It was inevitable that Elgar, Vaughan Williams and Walton were due for a 'comeback', but how fortunate that foreign-born conductors like Sir Georg Solti and André Previn should be in the forefront of the movement to establish them in their rightful places in the mainstream of international music.

ZUBIN MEHTA: *Turandot* by Puccini. With Joan Sutherland as Turandot, Montserrat Caballé as Liu, Luciano Pavarotti as Calaf, Peter Pears as the Emperor, Nicolai Ghiaurov as Timur, Pier Francesco Poli, Piero di Palma and Tom Krause as Ping, Pong and Pang, and Sabin Markov as the Mandarin. The London Philharmonic Orchestra, the John Alldis Choir and the Wandsworth Boys' Choir. LP: SET 561–3; Cassette: K2A2.

Faced with choosing a representative of the younger generation of conductors – the brilliant group which includes Abbado, Muti, Mehta,

Ozawa etc. – I fell back on a favourite work, magnificently conducted by a born Puccinian (born in India), Zubin Mehta. Puccini's black fairy tale too often fails on stage because of inferior pantomimish (British style) production, but it has been more fortunate on disc. Never more fortunate than here, however, for Mehta, with a fire worthy of de Sabata, electrifies his orchestra and cast to reach stupendous heights. As Rodney Milnes wrote in *Opera* (November, 1973), his conducting is 'beyond criticism', his interpretation 'muscular, dramatic, rhythmically urgent and utterly free of spurious sentiment.' He inspired Joan Sutherland, whom many feared in advance to be miscast, to achieve a total triumph, while the miscasting – as, again, it seemed in advance – of Caballé as little Liu also proved inspired after initial misgivings about the weight of her voice. Oddly, Peter Pears is not totally convincing. Lesser artists have made a much more convincing very old Emperor.

Yet this set stands ultimately on the triple pillars of conductor, orchestra and choir, and, as the supreme importance of the conductor in opera has been stressed in this book, let the last word be Mehta.

Select Bibliography

Including those works already acknowledged in the Introduction

BEECHAM, Sir Thomas. *A Mingled Chime* (Hutchinson, 1944)

BERLIOZ, Hector. *Evenings in the Orchestra*: Editor, David Cairns (Penguin Books, 1963)

BERLIOZ, Hector. *Memoirs*: translated by R. and E. Holmes (two volumes, London, 1884). Translated and edited by David Cairns (one volume, Gollancz, 1969)

BLOM, Eric. *Grove's Dictionary of Music and Musicians*, 5th edition (Macmillan, 1954)

CARSE, Adam. *The Orchestra in the 18th century* (Heffer, 1940)

CARSE, Adam. *The Orchestra from Beethoven to Berlioz* (Heffer, 1948)

DEL MAR, Norman. *Richard Strauss* (three volumes, Barrie and Rockcliff/ Barrie and Jenkins, 1962–72)

ELLEY, Derek: Editor. *International Musical Guide 80* (Trantivity Press, 1979)

GASTER, Adrian: Editor. *International Who's Who in Music and Musicians' Directory*, 8th edition (International Who's Who in Music, 1977)

JACOBS, Arthur: Editor. *British Music Yearbook 1980* (A. and C. Black, 1979)

JACOBS, Arthur: Editor. *New Penguin Dictionary of Music* (Penguin Books, 1977)

JACOBSON, Bernard. *Conductors on Conducting* (Macdonald and Jane's, 1979)

KENNEDY, Michael. *Barbirolli – Conductor Laureate* (McGibbon and Kee, 1971)

NEWMAN, Ernest. *The Life of Richard Wagner* (Cassell, 1976: the four volumes originally appeared separately from 1933)

PREVIN, André: Editor. *Orchestra* (Macdonald and Jane's, 1979)

RAYNOR, Henry. *The Orchestra* (Robert Hale, 1978)

REID, Charles. *Malcolm Sargent* (Hamish Hamilton, 1968)

ROBINSON, Peter. *Karajan* (Macdonald and Jane's, 1977). He has since written *Stokowski* and *Solti* in the same series.

ROSENTHAL, Harold, and John Warrack. *The Concise Oxford Dictionary of Opera* (2nd edition, Oxford University Press, 1979)

SACHS, Harvey. *Toscanini* (Weidenfeld and Nicholson, 1978)

SCHOLES, Percy A. *Oxford Companion to Music* (Oxford University Press, 1970)

SCHONBERG, Harold C. *The Great Conductors* (Gollancz, 1968)

SHORE, Bernard. *The Orchestra Speaks* (Longman, 1938)

WOOLDRIDGE, David. *Conductor's World* (Barrie and Rockcliff, 1970)

Handbooks and periodicals etc.

Classical Music
Gramophone
Gramophone Classical Catalogue
Hi-Fi and Record Review
Opera
Music and Musicians
Penguin Stereo Record Guide, Second edition
Penguin Cassette Guide
Records and Recordings